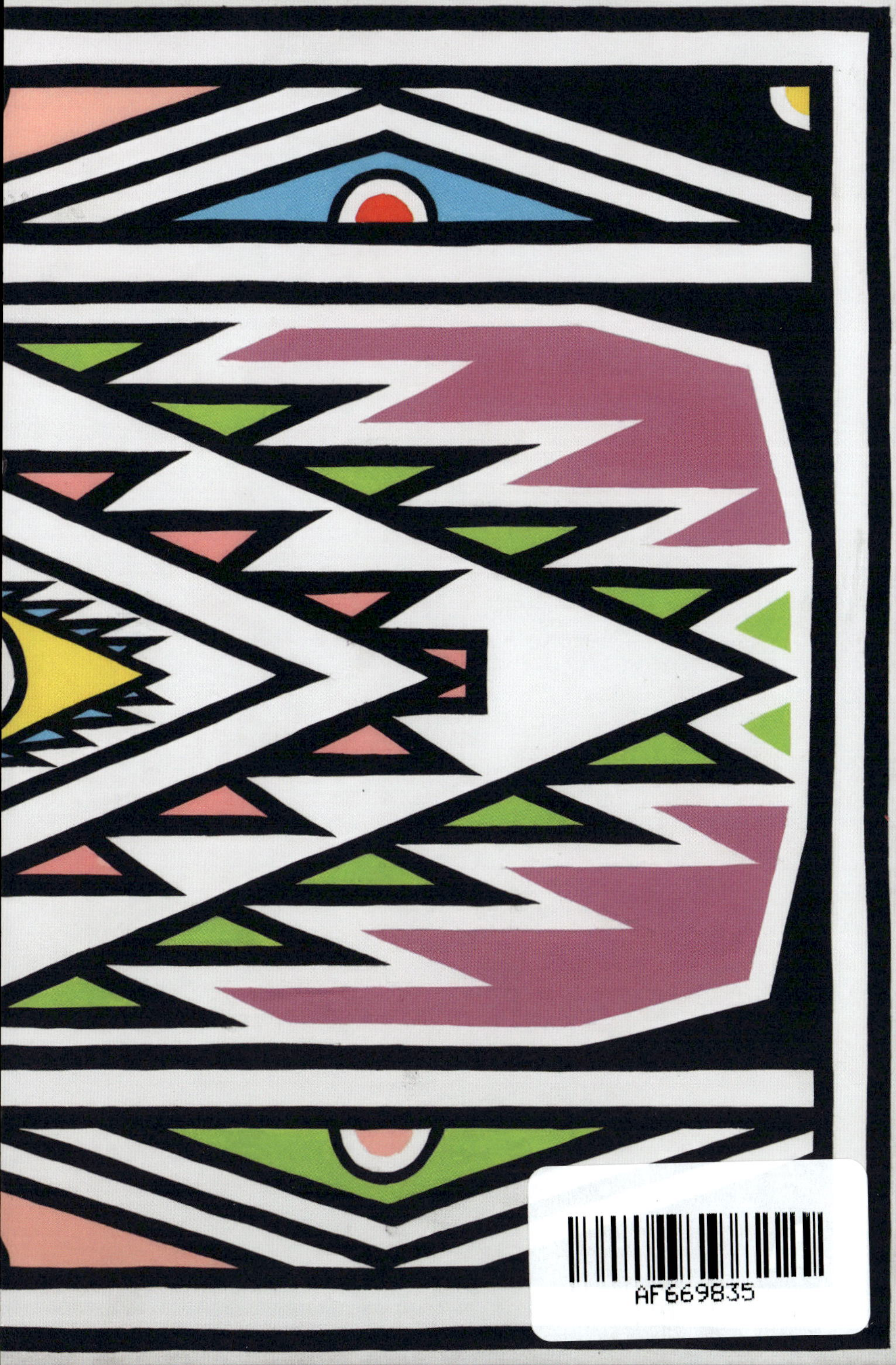

ESTHER MAHLANGU

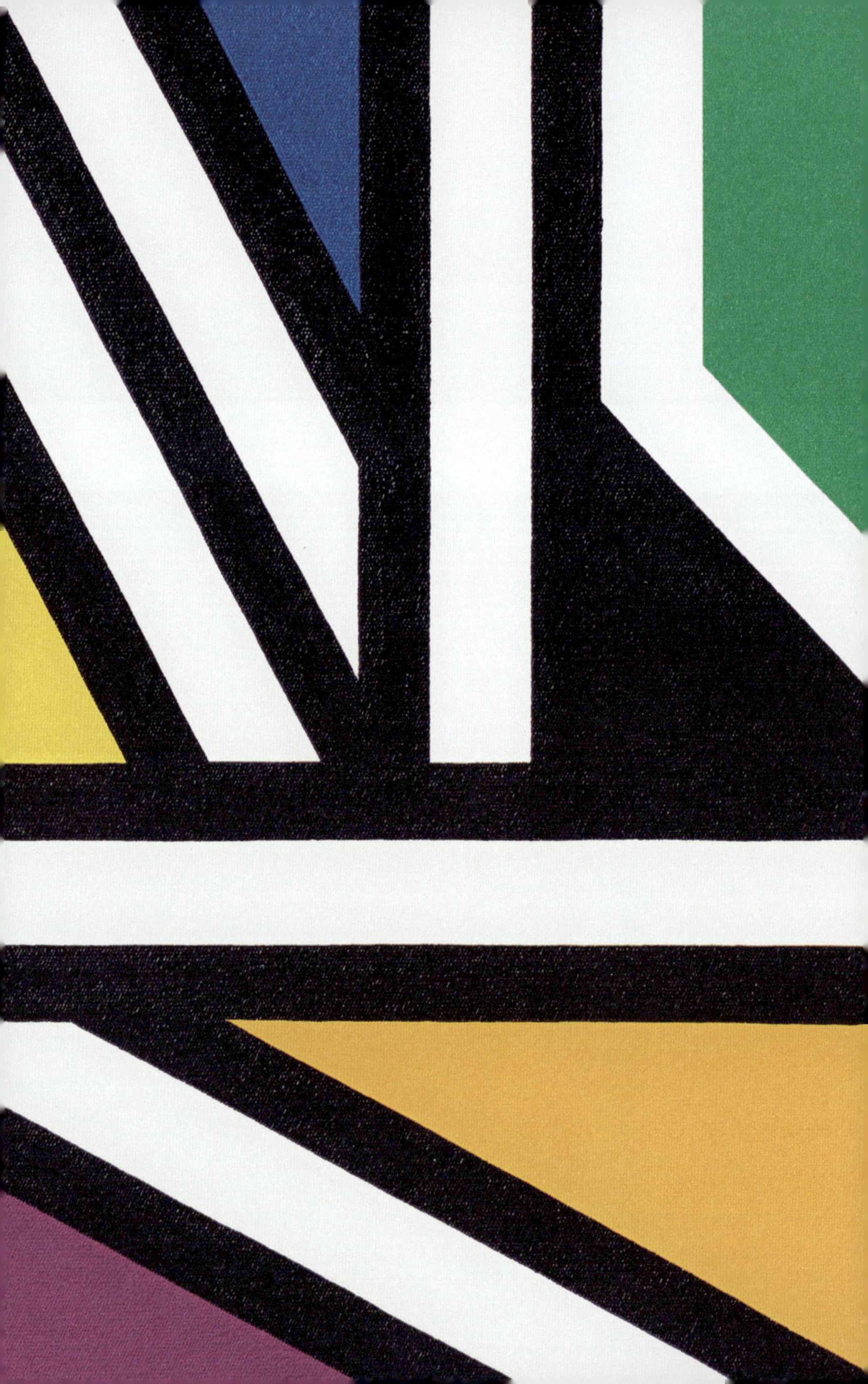

ESTHER MAHLANGU

TO PAINT IS IN MY HEART

THOMAS GIRST, AZU NWAGBOGU
AND HANS ULRICH OBRIST

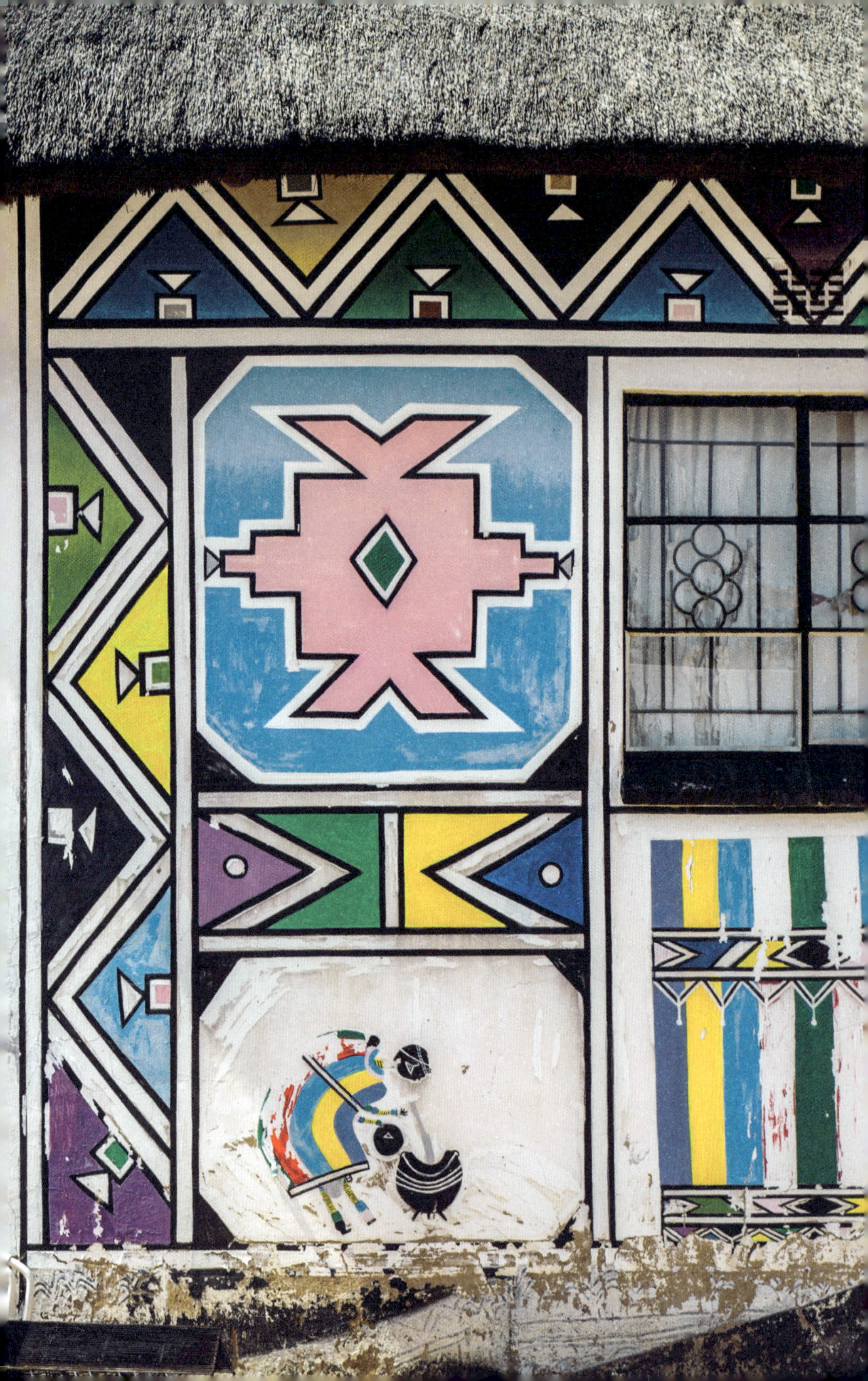

CONTENTS

FOREWORD 8
Nontobeko Ntombela

IN CONVERSATION 18
Thomas Girst, Azu Nwagbogu and Hans Ulrich Obrist, with Esther Mahlangu

'KGARI ESTHER MAHLANGU' 118
Pitika Ntuli

FASHIONING CULTURE 122
Thebe Magugu

ESTHER MAHLANGU: A BIOGRAPHY 134

SELECT BIBLIOGRAPHY 137

CONTRIBUTOR BIOGRAPHIES 138

ACKNOWLEDGMENTS 140

TEXT CREDITS 141

PICTURE CREDITS 142

As soon as
I start painting, everything
comes out on its own.

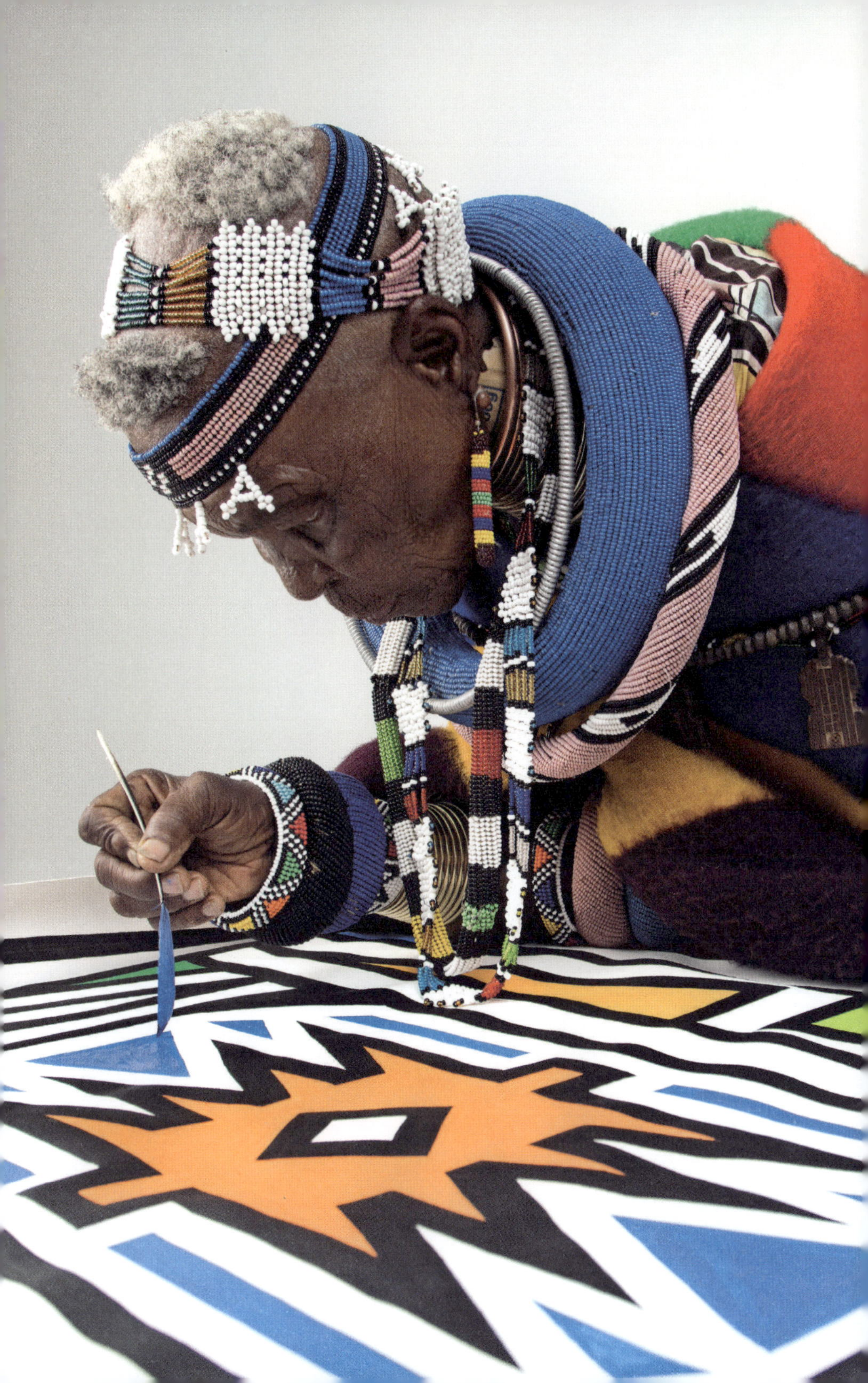

FOREWORD

Nontobeko Ntombela

I first encountered Esther Mahlangu's work in person at the Kunstmuseum Bochum, Germany, in 2007 during a bilateral curatorial project residency for young curators. Placed at the museum entrance, Mahlangu's mural stood alone, grand and proud. I immediately felt a connection to it.

This encounter was significant for me for two reasons. First, it embodied a moment and time when South Africa was still enjoying the lengthy euphoria of democratic dispensation and the way these celebrations were taking shape internationally. Secondly, seeing this mural in a place outside of South Africa prompted my own work on the history of Black South African women artists, which has stayed with me ever since.

Celebrated for her innovative practice, Mahlangu is widely recognized as one of the most influential artists across generations, both within and beyond South Africa. She has dedicated her life to sharing the colourful creativity of her Southern Ndebele culture with the world through wall paintings and beadwork, while also training others in these skills.

Mahlangu often tells the story of how she began her artistic journey at the age of ten, learning traditional techniques of Ndebele mural painting from her grandmother and mother, an experience that was a defining moment for her and set her on the path to becoming an artist. This self-awareness at such a young age is important given the fact that many historical accounts have only acknowledged artists of Mahlangu's generation once they were 'discovered' by the Western world. It is testament to Mahlangu's talent and its contribution to communal practice that she was able to embrace her destiny with such ease and bravery.

Over many years, her mural work has expanded over a wide variety of non-traditional surfaces, including found objects and automobiles, building upon this rich Ndebele tradition. Speaking about her innovative intuition, Mahlangu says: 'In everything I do, I'm trying to come up with my own designs. I'm trying to be innovative while sticking to the traditional colours, methods and styles.'[1]

Between 1980 and 1991, Mahlangu lived and worked at the Botshabelo Historical Village, Mpumalanga, an open-air museum of Ndebele culture, where she taught visitors to the centre about Ndebele life and practices. She has also established her own art school, teaching the details of Ndebele mural art as a way of giving back to the community and contributing to the preservation and development of traditional African knowledge systems.

This determination to teach demonstrates her desire to bestow on children the sustenance of indigenous knowledge. She is showing them how Ndebele mural painting can coexist with contemporary lifestyles while still retaining its historical and individual values. Mahlangu's commitment to this form of learning as key to the social development of children speaks to her resolve, optimism, resilience and belief in African knowledge systems and their evolution over time.

While her practice promotes her Ndebele heritage, it also opens up multiple interpretations. On many occasions, Esther Mahlangu has refuted fixed didactic explanations for her work. This has left many guessing at or wanting certain meanings, and some accusing her of lacking authenticity by not being bound by tradition. But what is tradition? While we know that mural painting has a long history in Africa, it is also known that the emergence of Ndebele mural painting in South Africa in the 1940s marked the end of a period of displacement and warfare. Firmly rooted in the cultural and political experiences of South Africa, as a social document Mahlangu's work not only reflects the legacy of land dispossession, the bitter rural conditions and erstwhile ethnic wars, but also holds up a mirror to her community's subversive, caustic commentary – full of the power of invention, wit and courage.

How, then, do we consider Mahlangu's work in this light? How might we understand that the multidimensional form and process of Mahlangu's intellectual project lies within the space of accessibility and inaccessibility, simplicity and complexity? How do we avoid falling into the trap of believing that it is impossible for a Black woman of her generation to be so daring, brave, visionary and innovative? How do we engage with these possibilities while retaining the generative work of promoting her culture and heritage to the world?

While so much has been said about Esther Mahlangu's mastery and brilliance, there is limited engagement with the intricacies that characterize her work's uniqueness, radicality and expansiveness. Writings about Mahlangu need to operate beyond wanting to explain her work to the world. Rather, we must seek new perspectives.

The mix of interviews, quotes, poetry and an essay discussing her work and Ndebele culture in relation to fashion that is found in this book – with contributions from Thomas Girst, Azu Nwagbogu, Hans Ulrich Obrist, Pitika Ntuli and Thebe Magugu – offers a different approach, prompting a reconsideration of the work of this national icon that might be the beginning of something alternative to what we already know. Her work continues to foster incredible creativity that will hopefully encourage new perspectives for many years to come.

1. *Esther Mahlangu: Indigenous Lines*, South African Department of Arts and Culture, Cape Town, 2019.

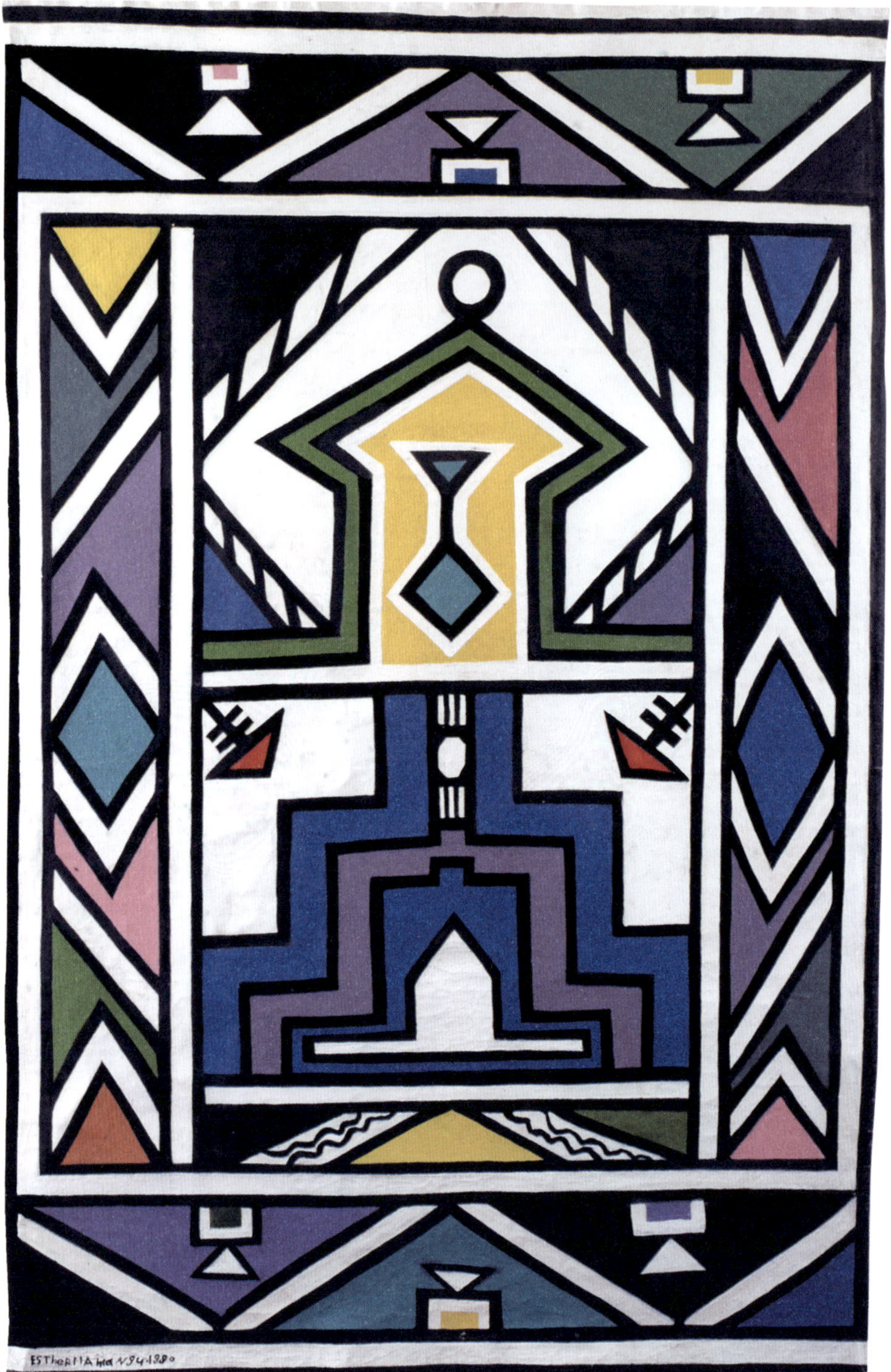

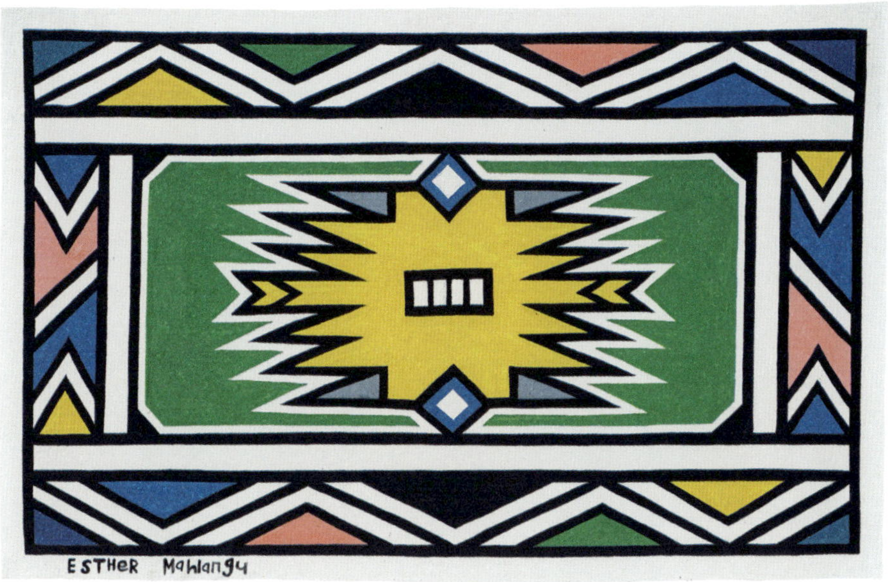
ESTHER Mahlangu

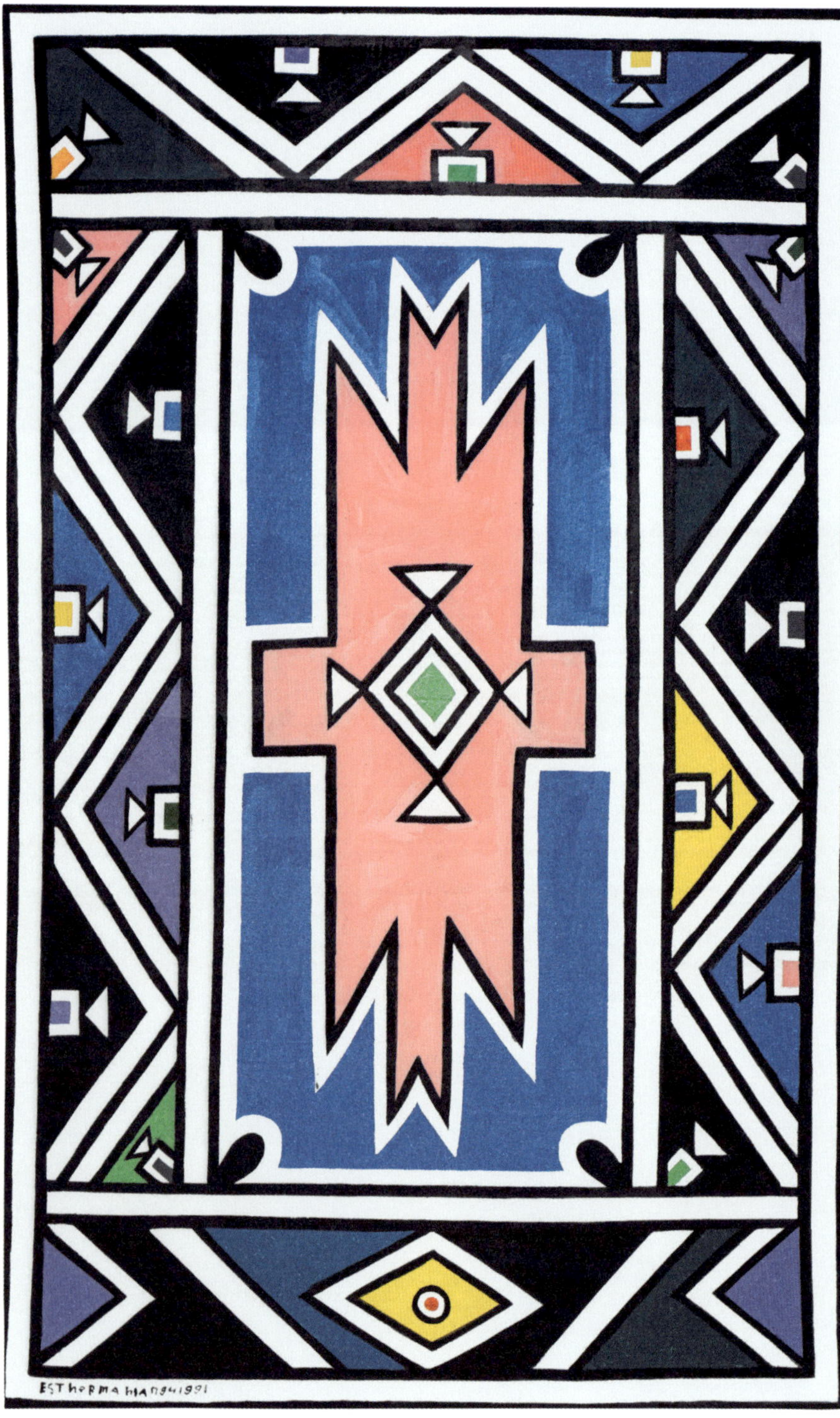

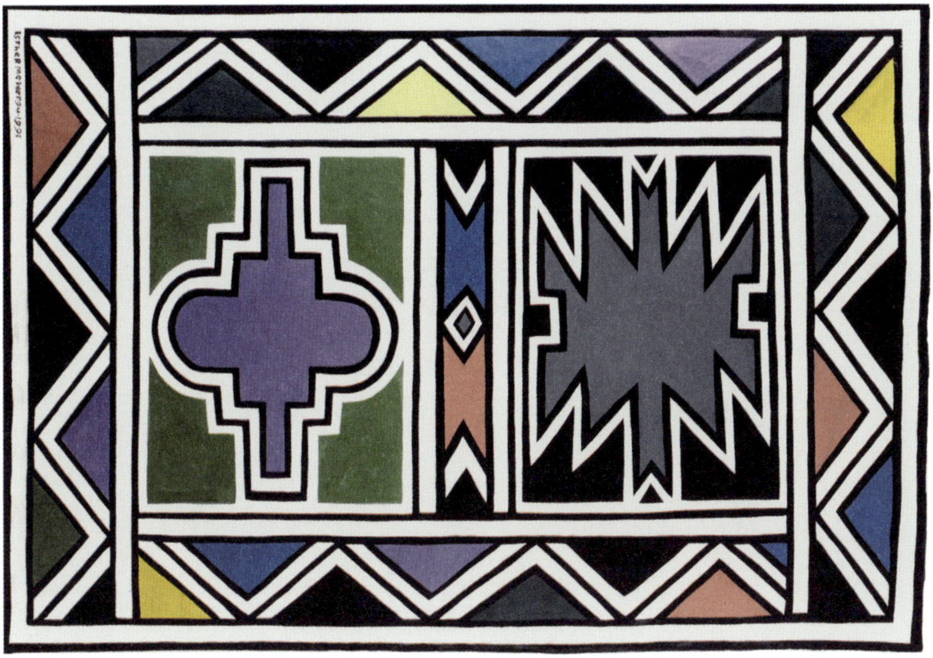

I painted the car like a wall.
And for the Ndebele people, if you
begin to paint a wall it means … that
something big is going to happen.

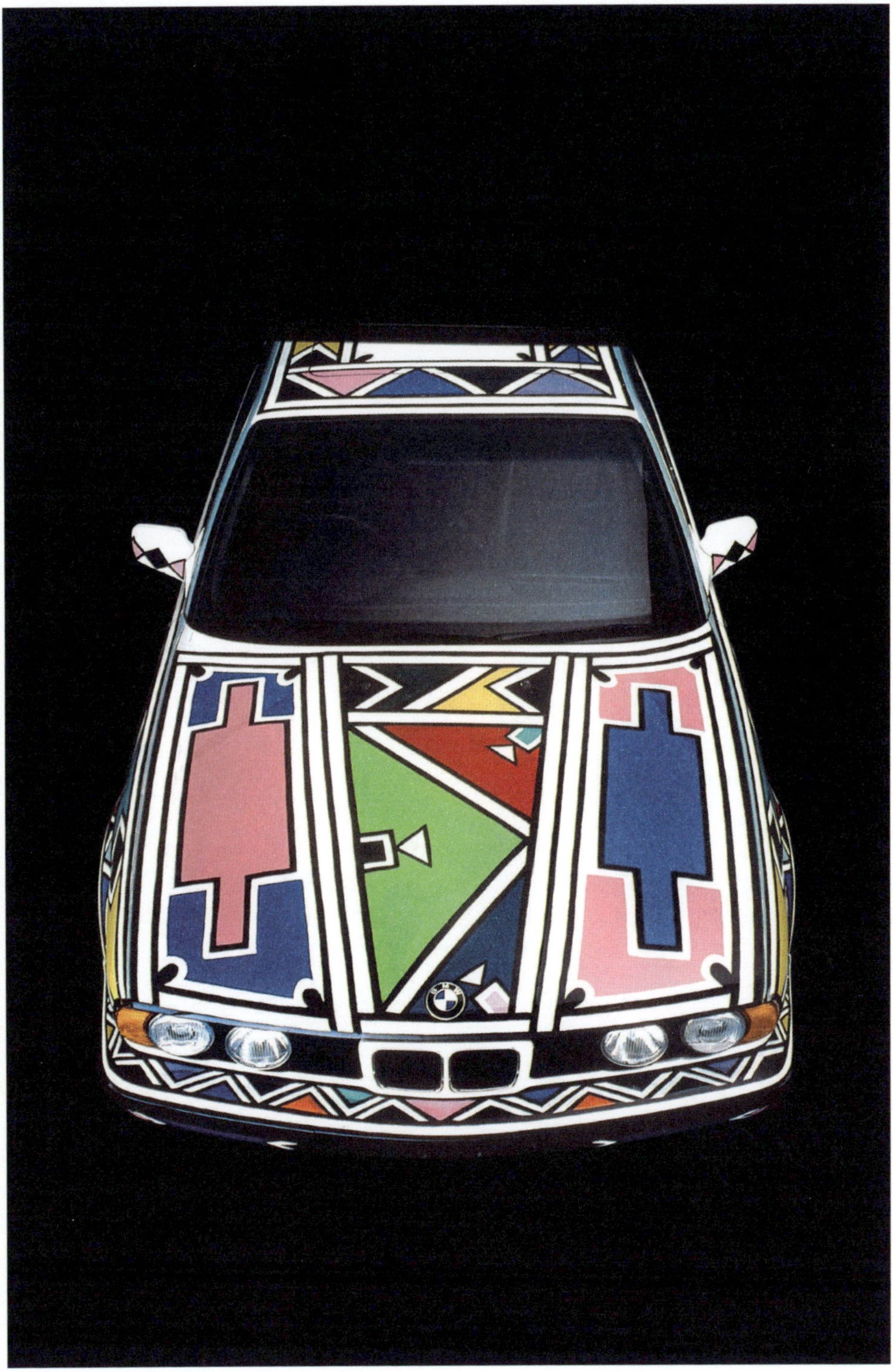

IN CONVERSATION

Thomas Girst, Azu Nwagbogu and
Hans Ulrich Obrist, with Esther Mahlangu

Dear Esther Mahlangu, thank you for welcoming us into your home. Would you share with us the origins of your journey as an artist?

I started creating art when I was a young girl. My family, particularly my mother and grandmother, were the ones who introduced me to Ndebele house painting. They used to paint the walls of our houses with our traditional designs. Those vibrant geometric patterns and bold colours fascinated me, and I wanted to create them too. As young girls, we used to play and imitate them, practising with resolve and showing off our skills. From a young age, we were being watched, and those with talent were encouraged and taught to refine their skills, not just with pencils but with brushes and traditional inks. My grandmother and mother were both skilled Ndebele artists. I would watch in awe as they painted the walls of our homes. It was like magic, and I couldn't resist the urge to join in.

Could you tell us a bit more about the colours you use in your artwork?

The process of gathering and creating colours is indeed challenging. We would find rich natural colours by the river and mix them with cow or other animal dung at home. The cow dung acts to hold the paint firmly, so it is not easily washed away by rain. These earth colours are the foundation of our traditional palette. 'Isarulsna', earth colours. They come from the land of our ancestors. They are shaped and coloured by time deep inside the earth's core. When I touch them, I feel closer to my ancestors!

These colours were primarily intended for outdoor use, such as on the facades of houses.

That's right. You see it all around. The colours were used outdoors, and despite challenges, we knew where to find the right materials by the river to create the colours we needed, whether white or any other hue.

At some point, you started using acrylic paint, which broadened your colour palette. Can you talk about when and why this happened?

The transition to acrylic paint was like walking with difficulty, it was a process. But these colours are all part of a memory, and learning to deploy them effectively is an ongoing journey. I've been working with colours for so long that the transition doesn't have a clear beginning.

Among all the different colours you've used, do you have a favourite?

I love all the colours because each one is unique and has its own charm. There isn't a specific colour I dislike. I appreciate the diversity in beauty. Each colour adds something different and, when combined, they create a harmonious melody. All the colours are related.

Talking about melodies, when looking at your work one can't help but think of music due to its lyrical and repetitive qualities.

Sometimes the colours speak like a song, they speak together and it's as if I am adding a melody with each

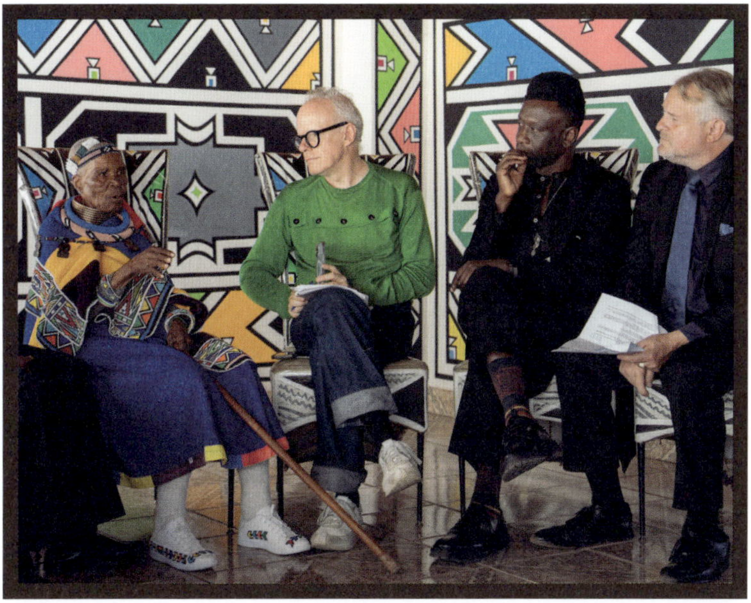

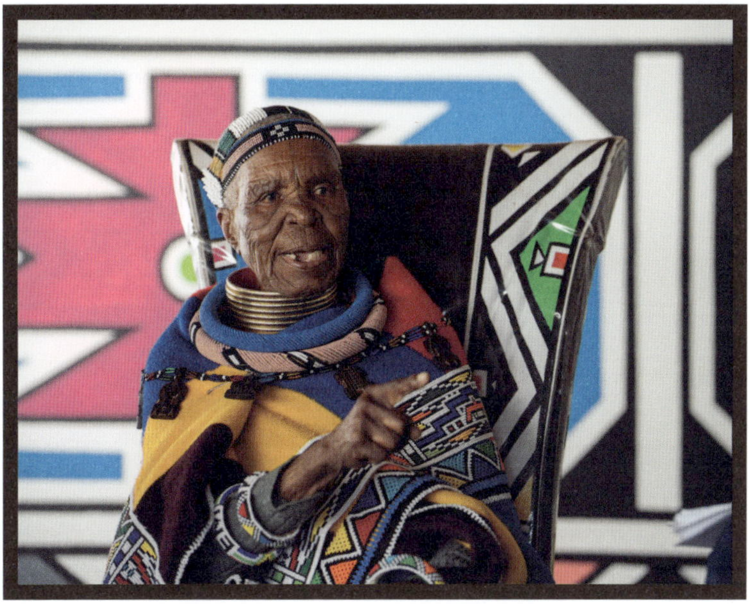

brushstroke. Some people see it as spiritual but, to me, it's about creating harmony with the colours, much like in music. I paint what is in my heart and what my heart tells me. I also paint what my brain tells me because I know it comes from deep down in the ancestral pools. When heart and mind agree, I know my spirit is in the right place. I paint to honour my ancestors!

Could you expand on the relationship between colour and music in your work?

The colours can sometimes quarrel, but it's important for them to harmonize. This harmony is akin to visual music, where each colour must complement the others to create a beautiful composition.

Reflecting on your own journey, if you could meet your ten-year-old self, just as you were starting to paint, what advice would you give to her from your current perspective?

I would tell any young child, including my younger self, to cherish their family and strive to progress beyond what I have achieved. It's important to guide them so they can live a better life, learning from our experiences.

You have a rich history tied to the Botshabelo Museum in Mpumalanga Province, a former mission station that also incorporated an Ndebele village as a kind of open-air museum, where you worked.

Yes, I volunteered at the Botshabelo Museum and it holds a special place in my heart. When we went there, the museum was already built, but there were no colours.

They were still plastering with mud. And then, after a while, they brought in the colours and said to us, here are the colours, here is the wall. This is your challenge. Bringing colour to the museum's walls, to create something vibrant and alive. That experience was like sowing seeds for the future, watching new generations walk in my footsteps.

In the process of painting, how did you learn to select and blend colours? Was this a skill that you developed over time?

We learned to paint from a young age, imitating the older generations. We would take small amounts of colour to practise on our own. You had to start painting with a feather right at the beginning. The process of selecting and blending colours is deeply connected to that. In the end, it is my mental balance that keeps me going, for with it I need no ruler to draw straight lines. I was taught early on the importance of balancing my emotions and my thoughts. Hence my motto: Heart, Mind and Spirit!

Your work is often described as a blend of abstract and figurative elements and the patterns have been linked to anything from mathematics to cosmology. Do specific colours in your work represent something beyond their aesthetic value?

Each colour has its own significance and beauty, and while some might search for deeper meanings, I focus on the composition as a whole. The colours I choose are about balance and harmony, and how

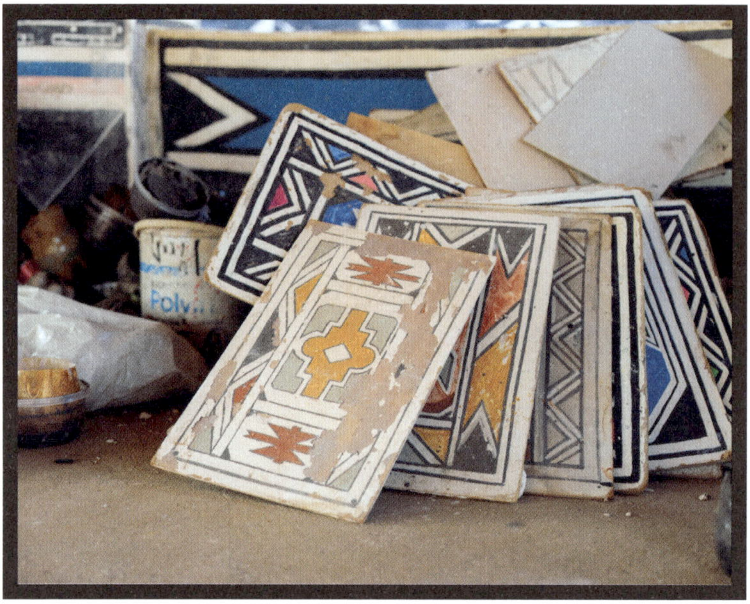

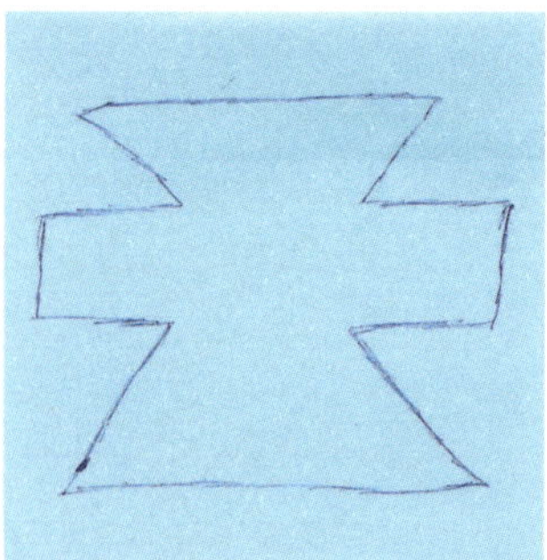

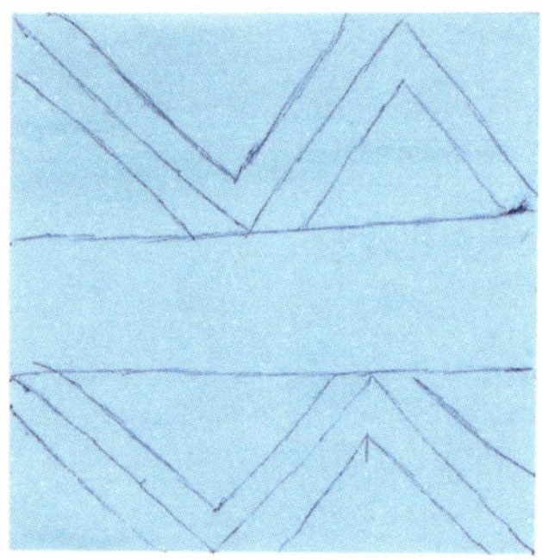

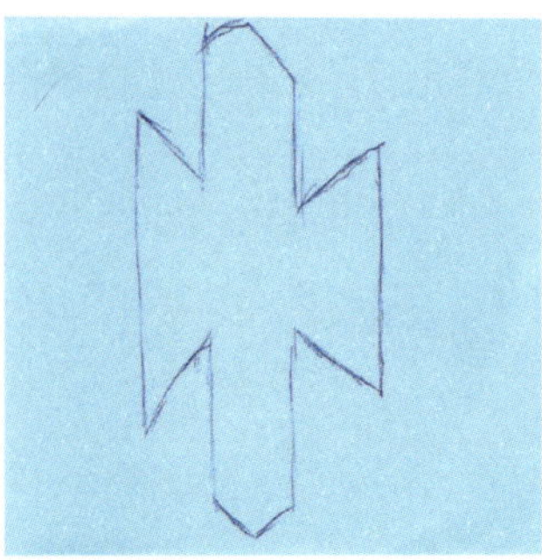

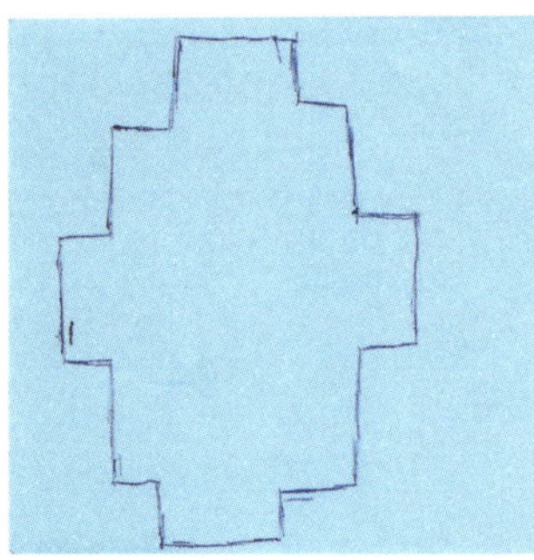

they come together to create the final artwork is what's most important.

Are you still able to find the same natural colours from the riverbanks as you did in the past?

The riverbanks are a source of a variety of colours, including blue. The natural environment provides a rich palette that continues to inspire my work and innovation in colour.

In your work, with its geometric forms and vibrant colours, there is mostly an absence of direct figuration or representation of people.

In my art, the progression and evolution of shapes and colours stand out. While you may not see huts or people, the art speaks in a different way. It's about moving forward and embracing a way of life that endures with us, a life that is rich with ancestral forces and abstract persuasion. These elements are present in my work, even as I have transitioned from traditional to modern mediums like acrylic.

Following up on that, how does the visual language of your geometric work connect to key life events or experiences? Does your work include symbolism that shifts depending on your personal experiences or broader societal changes?

The visual language in my work moves in a way that can represent experiences or evoke memories. When I create, it's as if I am rejoicing, and it feels like a celebration. The abstract forms might not directly depict events, but they are influenced by the rhythms and flows of life, including joys and challenges. I hold a feather in my hand, then something takes over and I draw a straight line. Then I'm fulfilled.

How do key life events, such as major societal transformations like Nelson Mandela's release from prison, influence your work? You have co-created a series of artworks inspired by some of his own sketches. Do these joyous events affect your choice of colours or inspire you to create something monumental?

While such events are joyous and significant, my art remains dedicated to my craft. Before apartheid we had body decorations. For instance, women would have a long tattoo from the forehead to the tip of the nose. We called it 'Umbobo'. Men designed their bicycles into sculptural forms. Because of migrant labour systems and farm work, those art forms declined and disappeared. My work seeks to remind me of who we were before the arrival of white people in our land. I focus on my work, and though the world around me may change, I am committed to the art form I have been practising for a lifetime.

You are considered a pioneer and innovator in Ndebele art. How do you see your pioneering work building upon what you've learned from your ancestors?

I have always been dedicated to my craft, and while I may be seen as a pioneer, I am simply carrying on the traditions that have been entrusted to me.

My innovations are a natural progression of the ancestral knowledge passed down through generations. We rejoice for those who have paved the way for us in life. We come from the earthly realm with joy because there is something that will help us, something desired by many.

There seems to be a deep gratitude for the support you've received in your artistic journey.

I am grateful to those who have helped me obtain the materials I need for my work, such as the quick-drying paints that have helped me achieve my artistic goals more efficiently. My journey has been one of collaboration and support from many people.

Could you reflect on your collaboration experiences and how they have shaped your work and relationships within your community?

The collaborations I've been a part of have always been harmonious. When I've encountered challenges or made mistakes, I've had supportive people who helped to guide me. These experiences have contributed to a rich and united working environment where we can all share our knowledge and grow together. My school, my passion for training and teaching young people to follow in my footsteps, is a way of being true to those who guided me as a child. It is me paying them back for what they taught me.

Can you tell us about the Ndebele sense of style and fashion? Is it a localized cultural expression or something unique to individual taste?

Ndebele culture is unique and loved by its people, just like other cultures cherish their heritage. We appreciate our traditions and the diversity within them. Our sense of style – it all comes from a mix of heritage, a blend of different cultures and traditions that represent our rich and diverse history. 'Ehhulwini' is a value system among the Ndebele, a form of recognition. Those who were present and those who were not present. Strength in the Ndebele culture is demonstrated through leadership and authority, creating a path forwards. This strength comes from our heart and spirit, and it is evident in our cultural practices.

Are there dreams you have at night that you can share with us? Dreams about your paintings, perhaps?

The paintings are always in my heart. I can never forget about the paintings. As for dreams, I normally forget them.

Could you share the story behind the colourful decoration of Ndebele houses and its relation to the history of the Ndebele people?

The tradition of painting our houses in bright colours has its origins in our history where, during a time of conflict, the Ndebele people were forced into hiding in a cave. It was there, while besieged and running out of food, that they planned for the future and the safety of their homes. Each year, we pay tribute to those who lived in that cave and the ideas that emerged there.

In 1989 you participated in the exhibition 'Magiciens de la terre' at the Centre Pompidou in Paris, where your

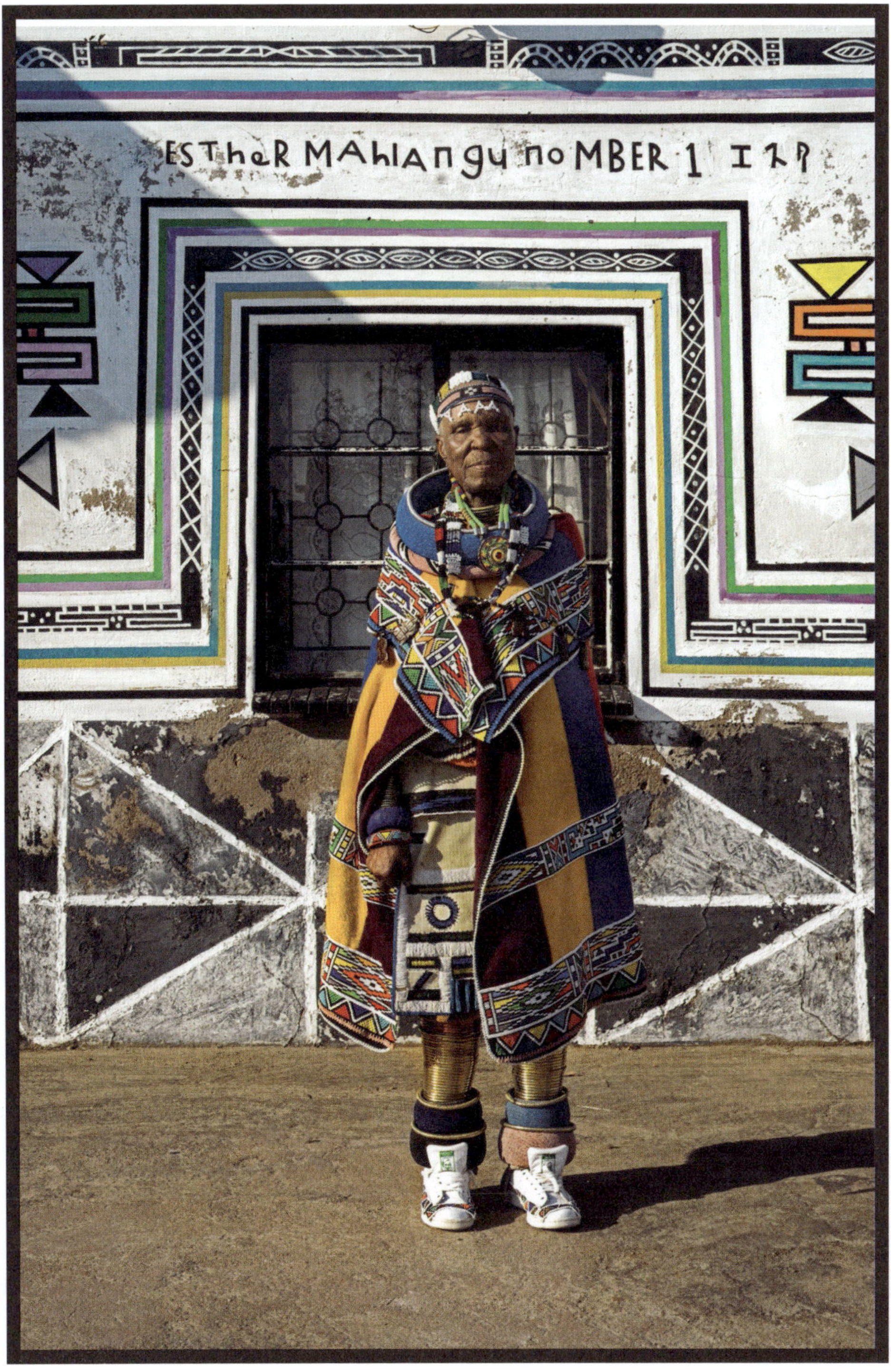
ESTheR MAhlAngu noMBER 1

work was taken out of its traditional context for the first time. Can you reflect on that moment and the significance of presenting your art in a new environment?

That moment in 1989 was pivotal. When my work was displayed in Paris, it was a completion, a sense of accomplishment. To share our culture with the world and see it appreciated outside of its local context was a joyous experience.

How do you find painting on a wall different from painting on a canvas, and how did you feel seeing your work in a Western context like Paris?

Painting a wall involves standing and dealing with gravity, while painting on a canvas allows for relaxation and creativity as you can sit down flat on the ground or at a table. Seeing my work in Paris, away from its local context, was a moment of joy – beautiful and spectacular. It was a recognition of the completion of something significant and a reflection on that accomplishment.

Having travelled the globe, do you have a favourite city? Were you inspired by other artists or architecture in the places you visited?

I don't have a favourite city. I feel welcomed wherever I go and remember fondly the places where I was happy and the people who treated me well. Wherever I am treated with kindness, where there is a feast and a celebration, that place uplifts my spirit. It's so good to go to any country and experience the variety of cultures. Each one is different and interesting. Recently, I visited Johannesburg, and the experience was filled with fun and absolute joy. It's these moments of connection and shared happiness that stand out and make everything worthwhile. Everything I did came from my heart. I travelled to all the places and everything to me is special because I did it with love.

How important is time to you?

Time is very important. You must be punctual! Punctuality is a priority for me.

What can make you angry?

I get mad at people who lie. I hate liars; they're like water and oil to me. We don't mix.

What brings you the most joy in life?

The most interesting thing to me is the Ndebele tradition and the paintings. It's my culture that makes me happy.

People who bring joy and love seem to be naturally drawn to you. How do you feel about being a source of inspiration and positivity for others?

I am delighted by those who come with positivity. It's a joy when they carry that love back to their homes. It's not the names you give to others that make you be remembered, but the genuine care from those who love you.

Do you have a favourite joke?

I don't really have a joke to tell. I guess it's amusing when Ndebele tradition comes into play with modern habits, like women wearing trousers!

What is your favourite food?

I love traditional dishes like 'lude', which is a green vegetable we grow in the wet fields, and 'msobo', a jam made from the nightshade plant. These are the types of food we eat.

What is art to you? Do you have a definition of it?

Art is something that brings joy and pride when I look at it. When others see my art and feel hope or happiness it feels like a celebration, a ceremony of life's beauty. I laugh with myself sometimes when I work. I refuse to be distracted. I laugh inside my heart and mind. To those who want something from me, I offer hope. When I look at myself and my work, I see happiness and joy, like the early morning. It's about sharing that feeling of contentment and celebration with others.

If you hadn't become an artist, what else do you think you might have become?

I haven't really thought about that. It never crossed my mind to be anything other than an artist.

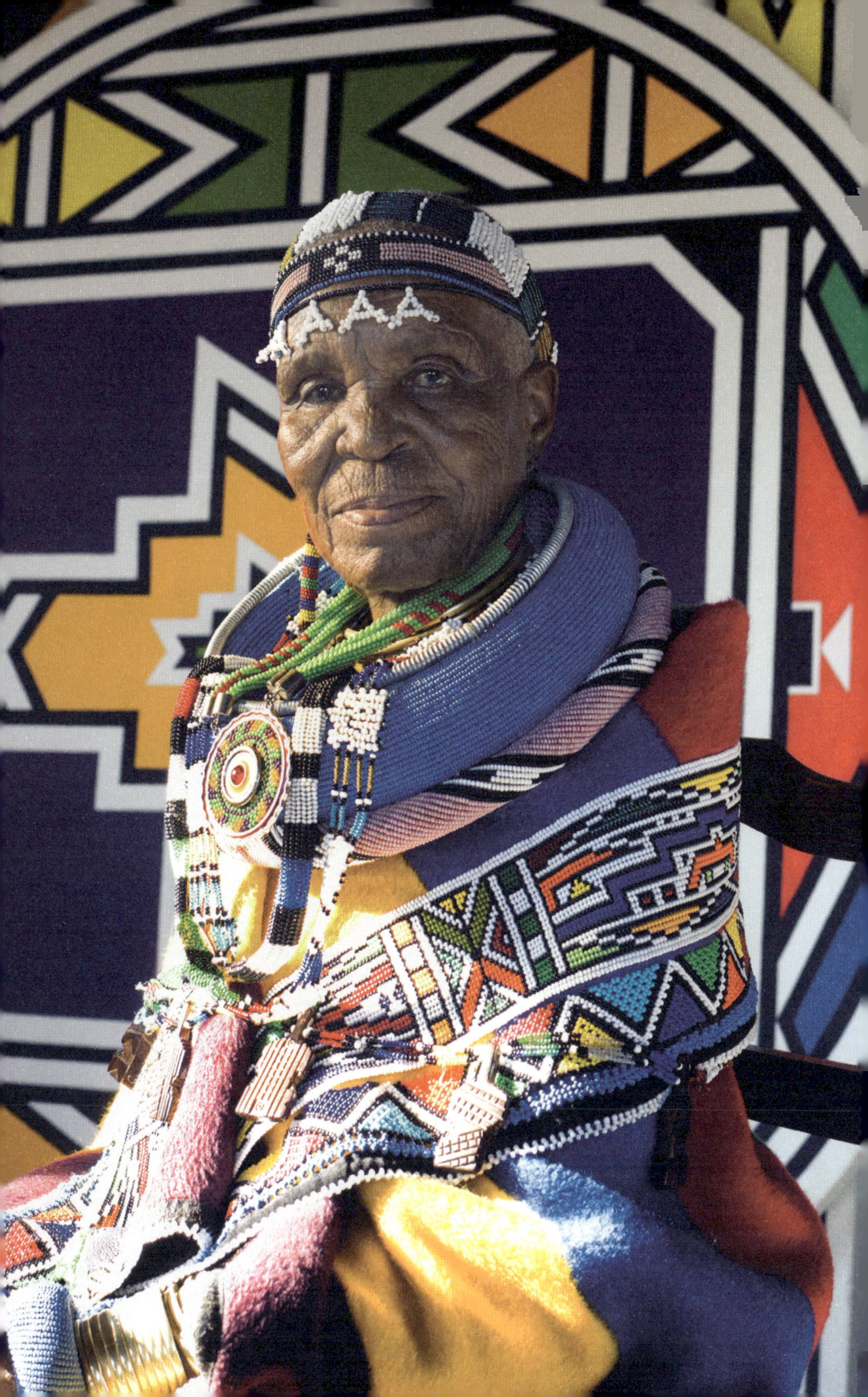

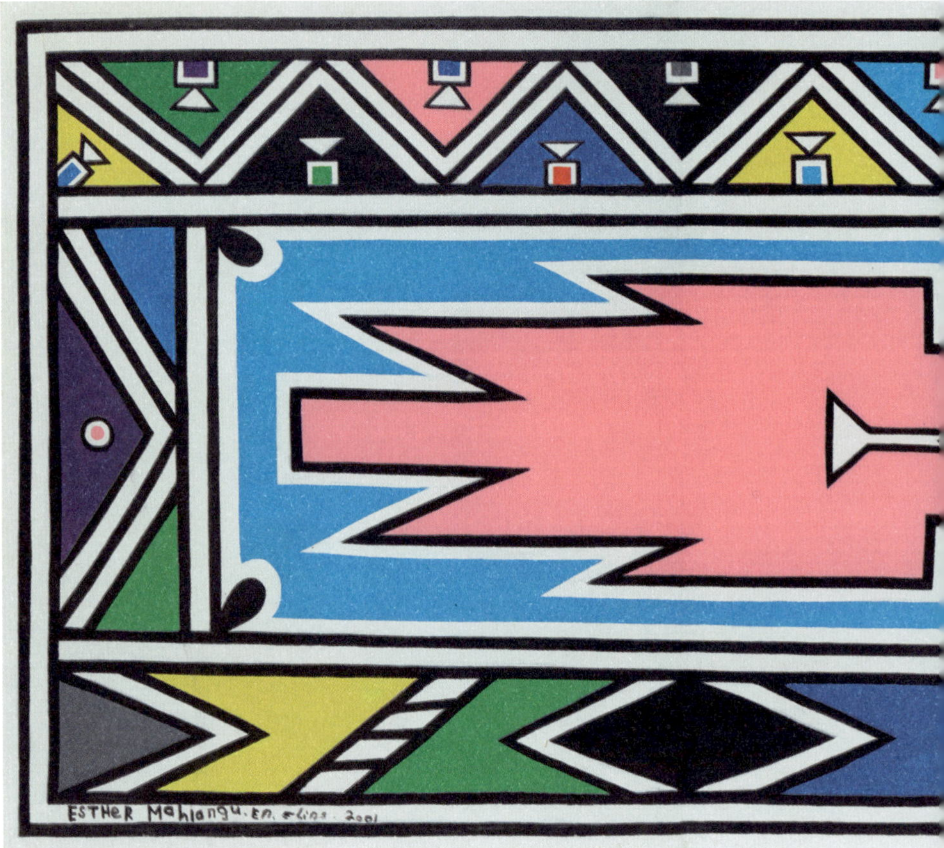
ESTHER Mahlangu. EN. elias. 2001

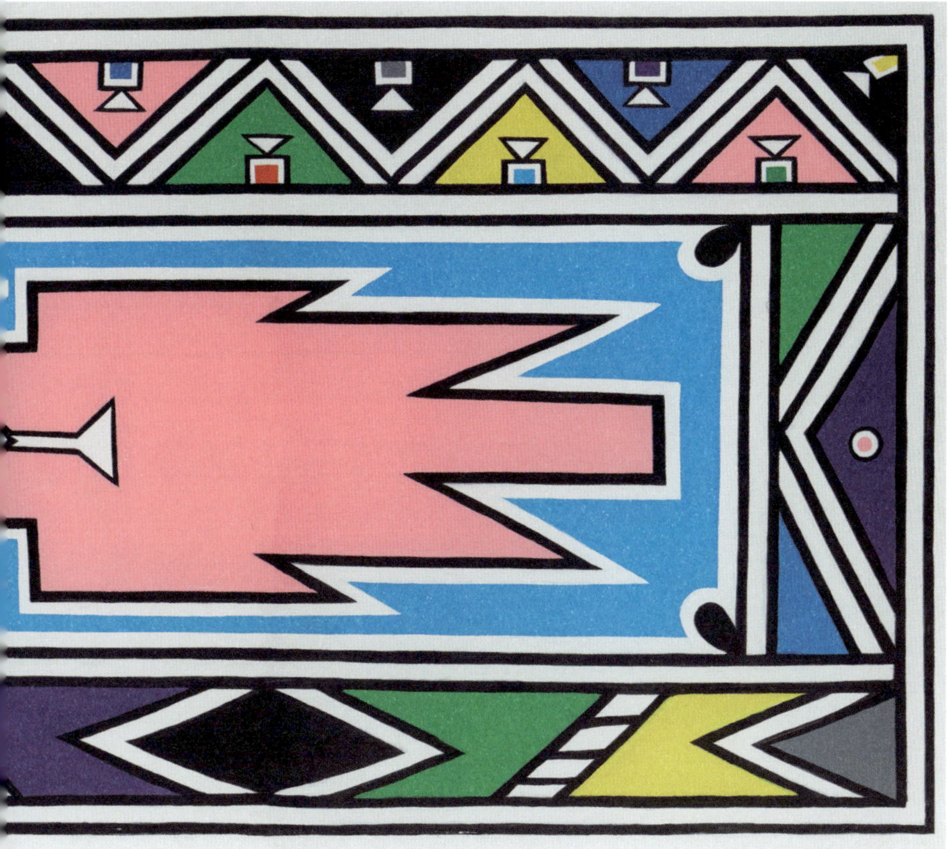

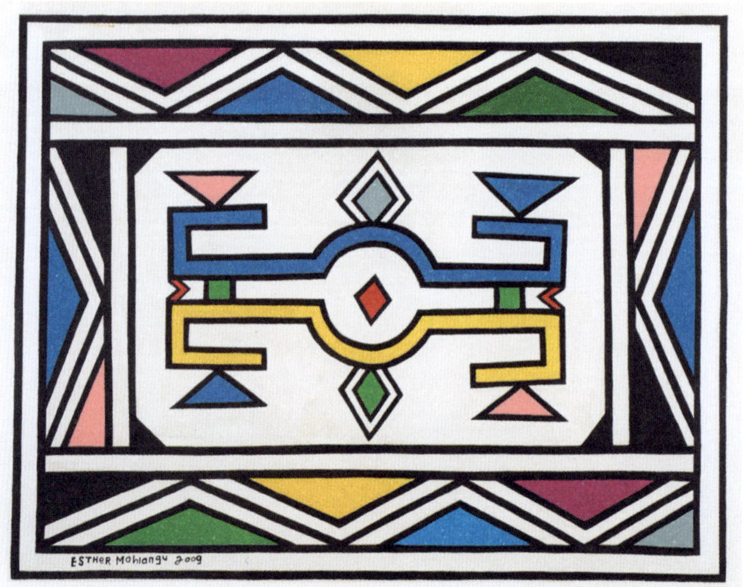
ESTHER Mahlangu 2009

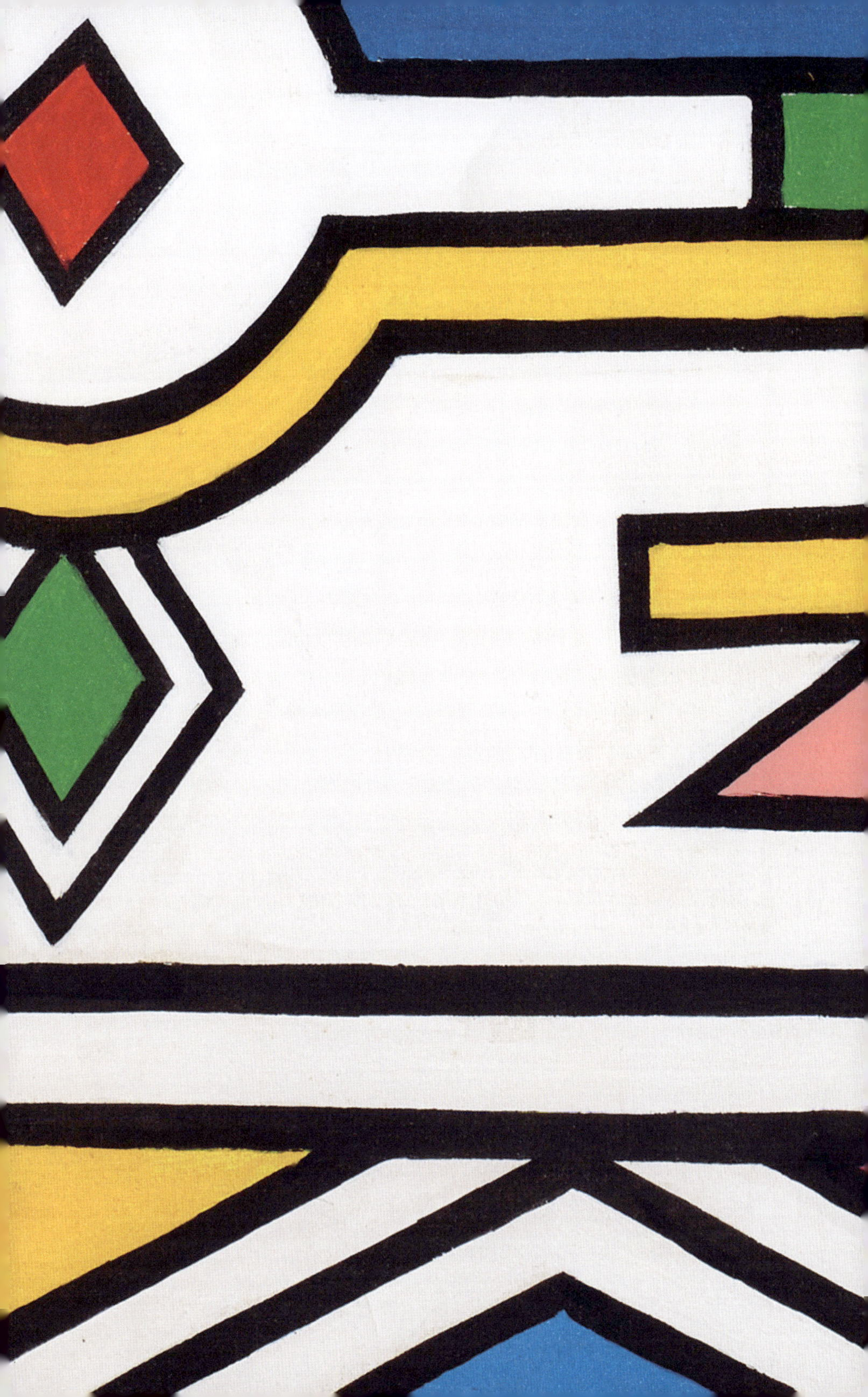

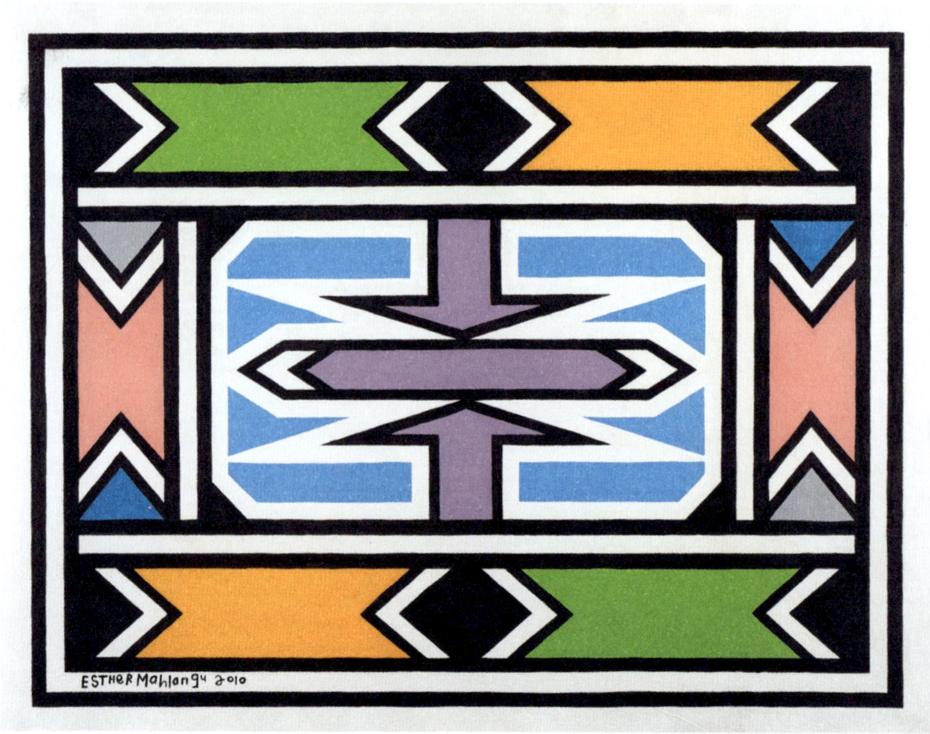
ESTHER Mahlangu 2010

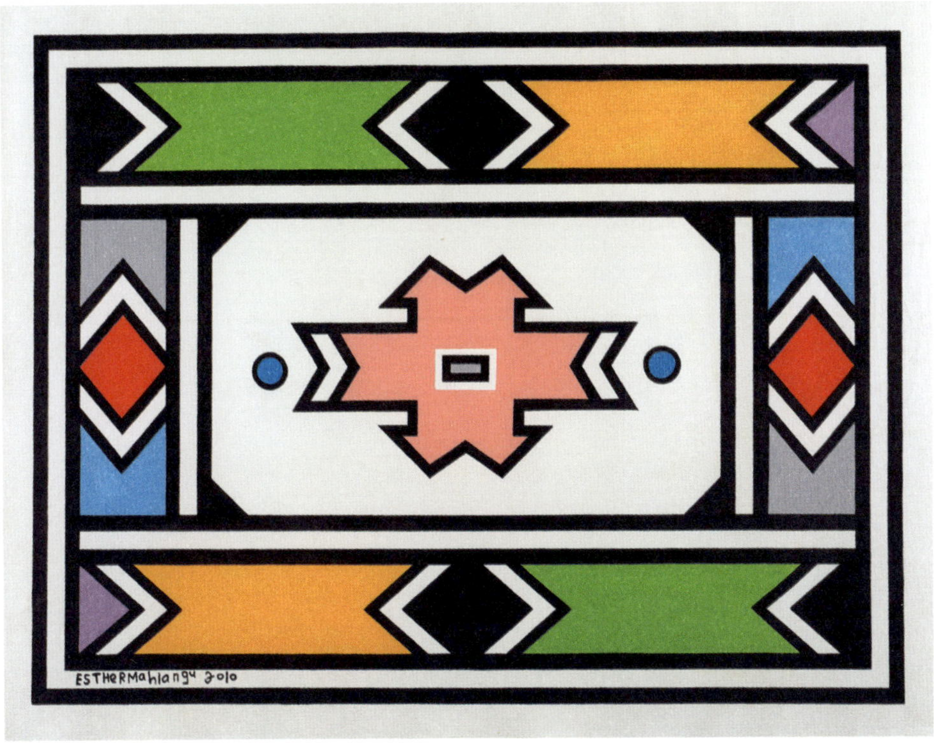
ESTHERMahlangu 2010

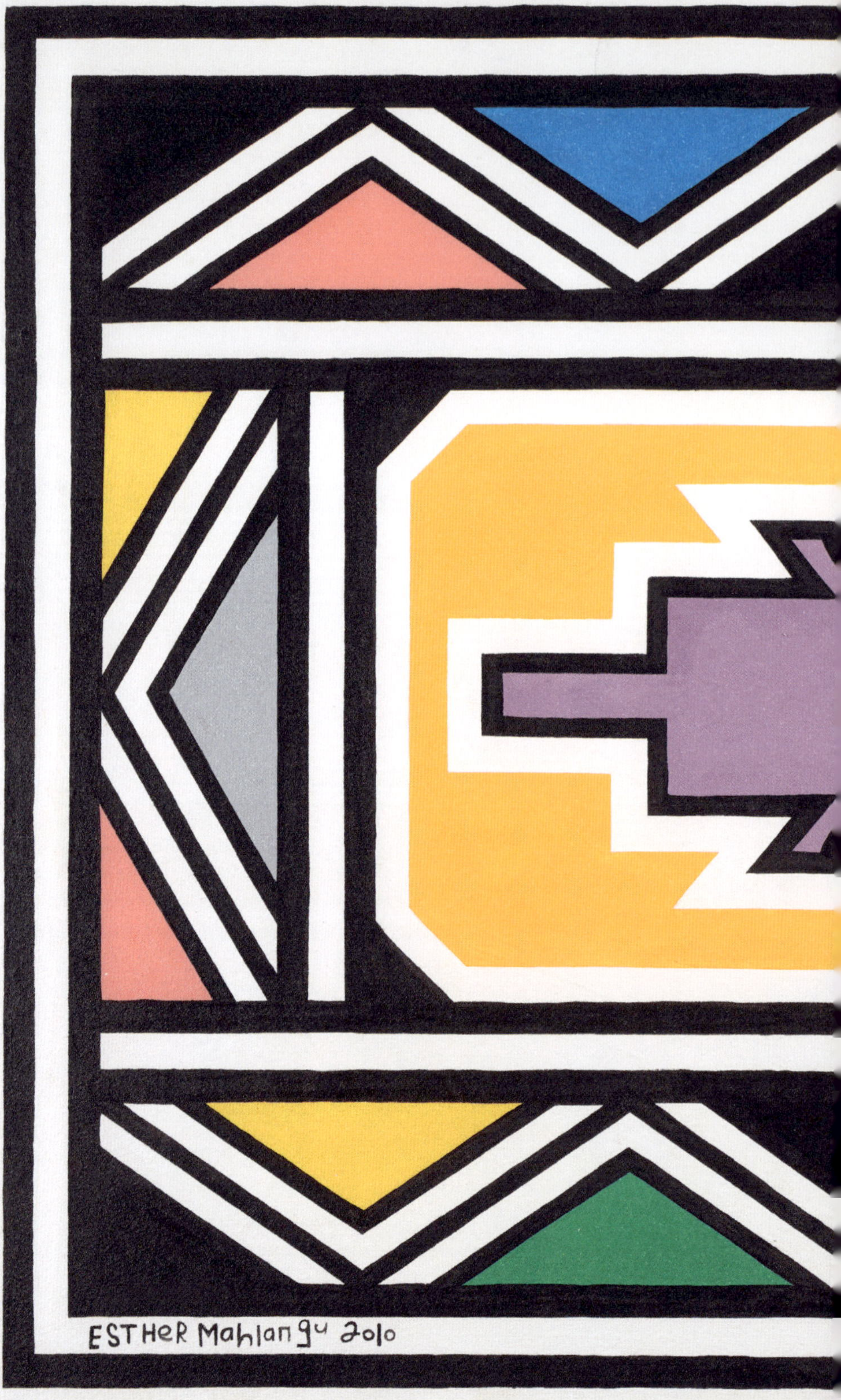
ESTHER Mahlangu 2010

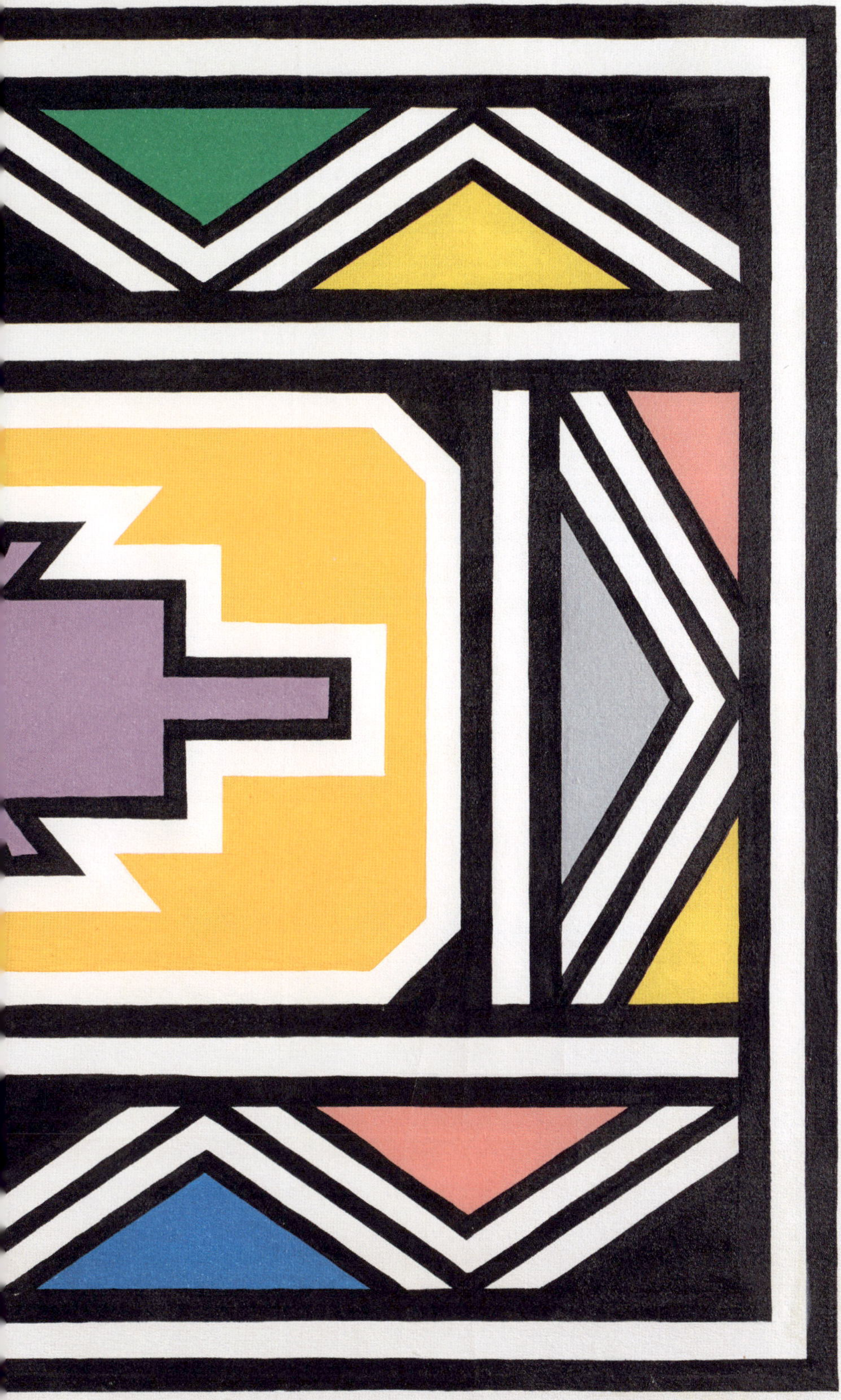

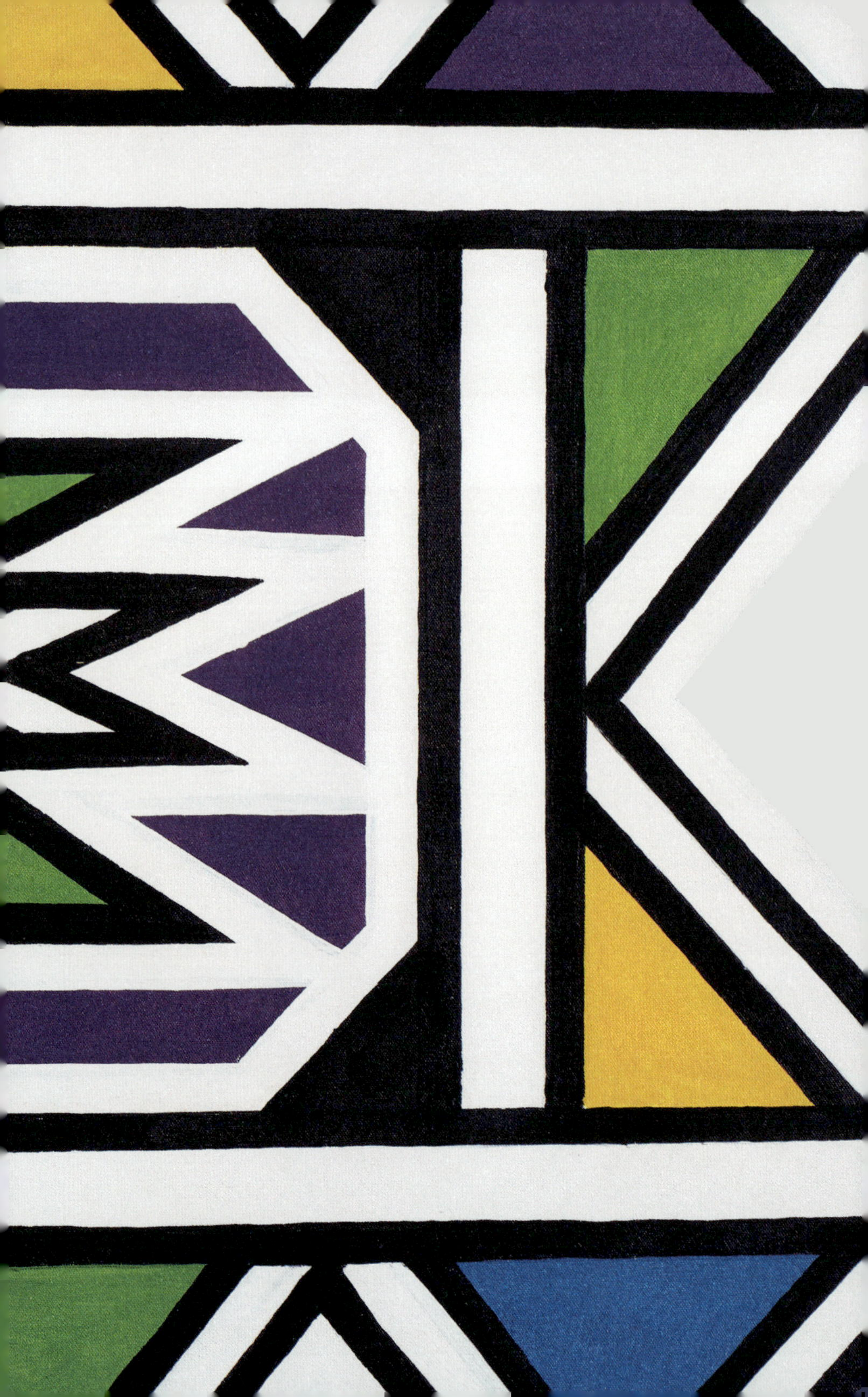

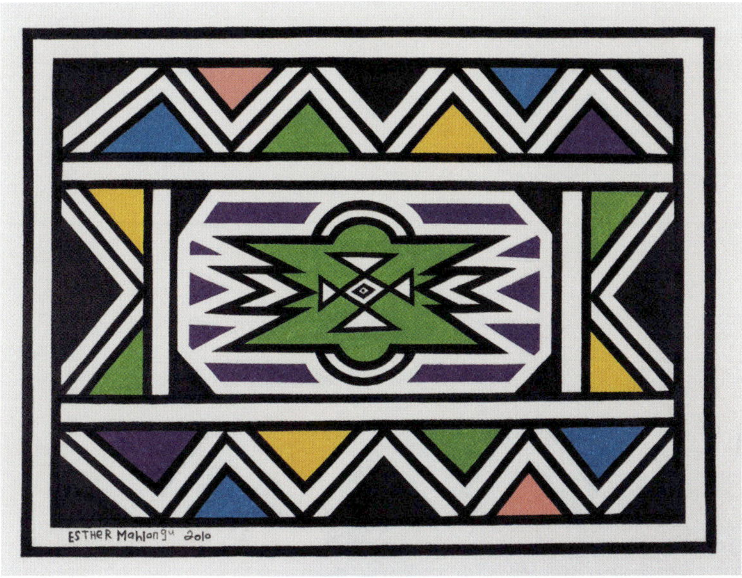

Painting is in my blood. Nothing will ever stop me painting and drawing. I will paint and draw until I die.

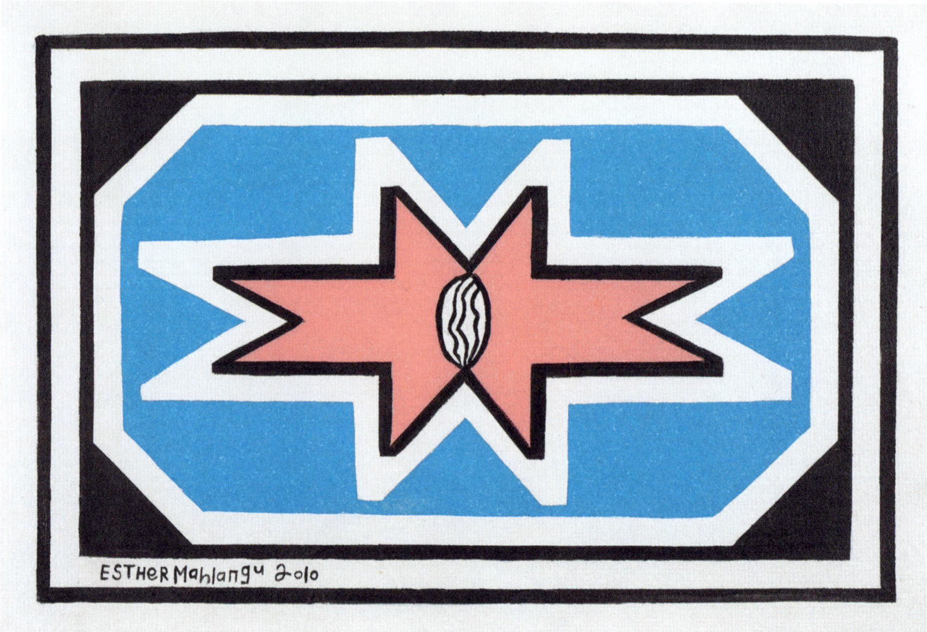
ESTHER Mahlangu 2010

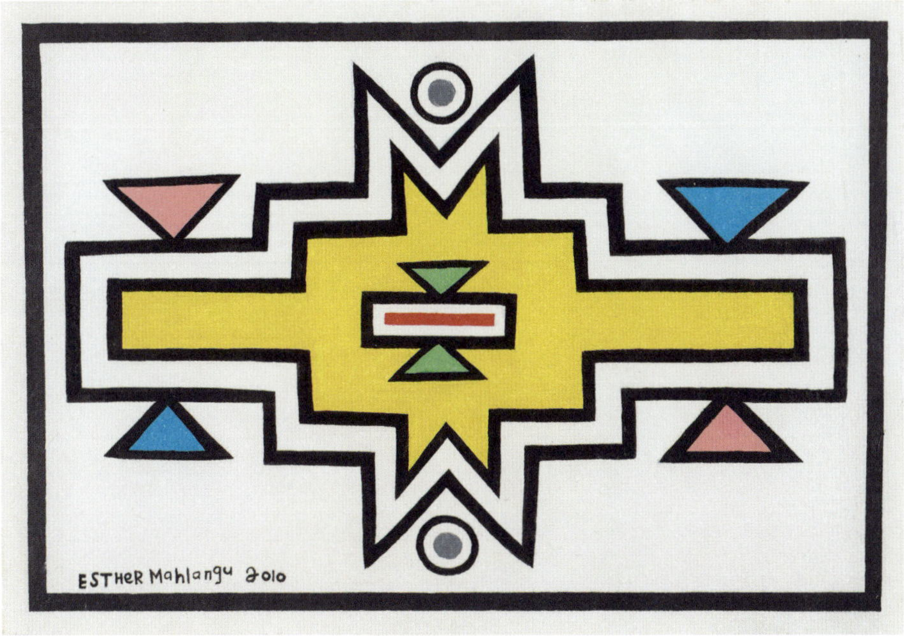
ESTHER Mahlangu 2010

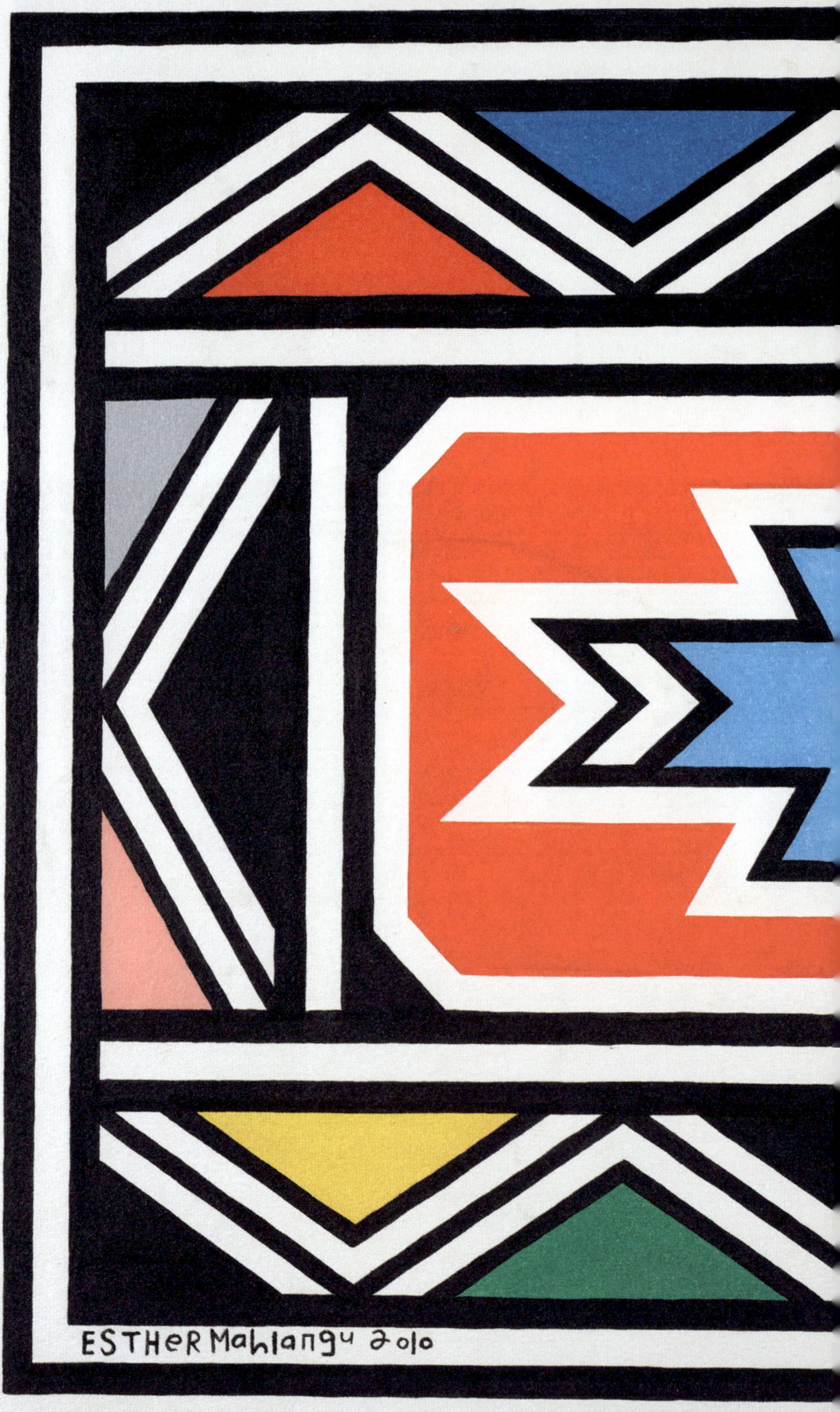
ESTHER Mahlangu 2010

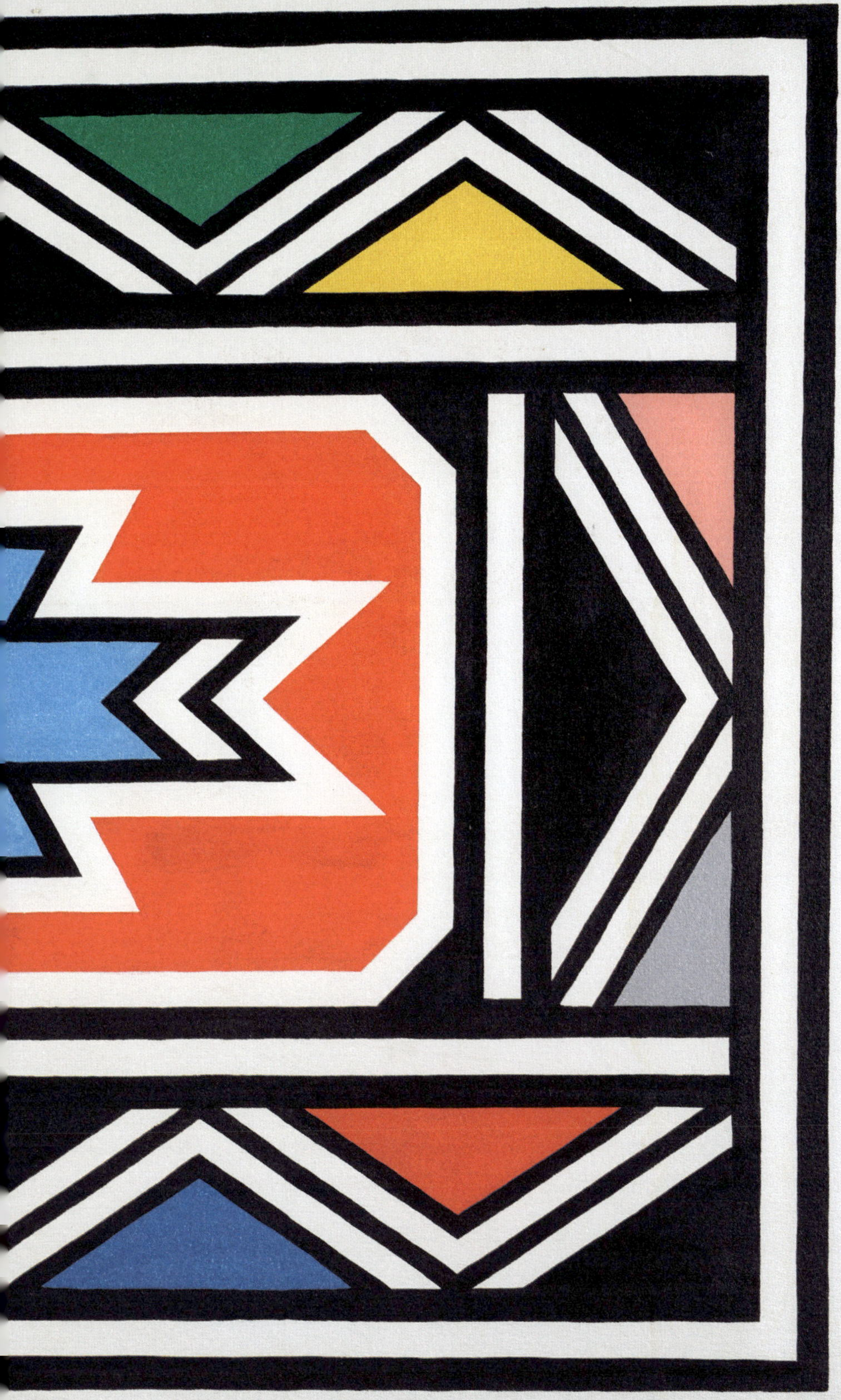

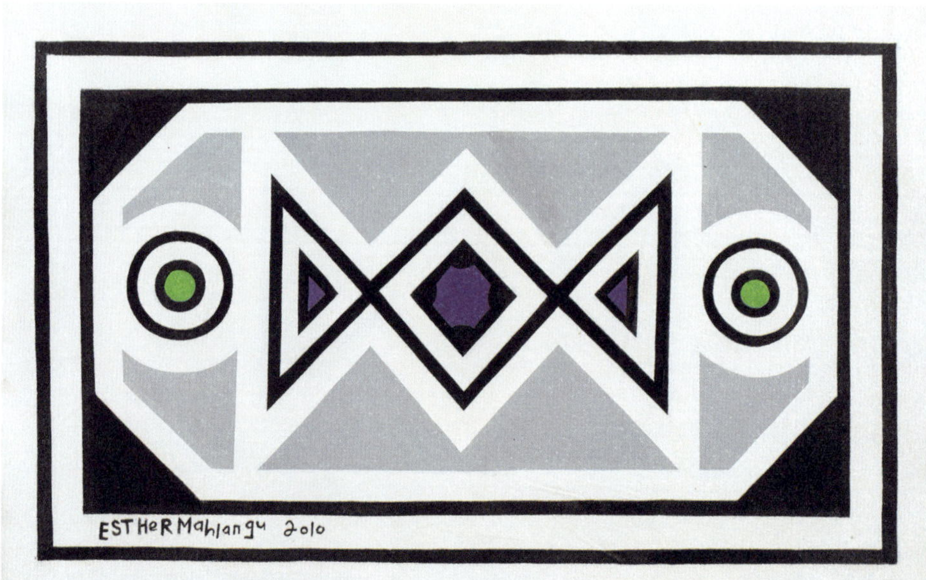

I use the image of the razor blade ('itjhefana') in my work a lot ... it plays such a monumental role in our daily lives.

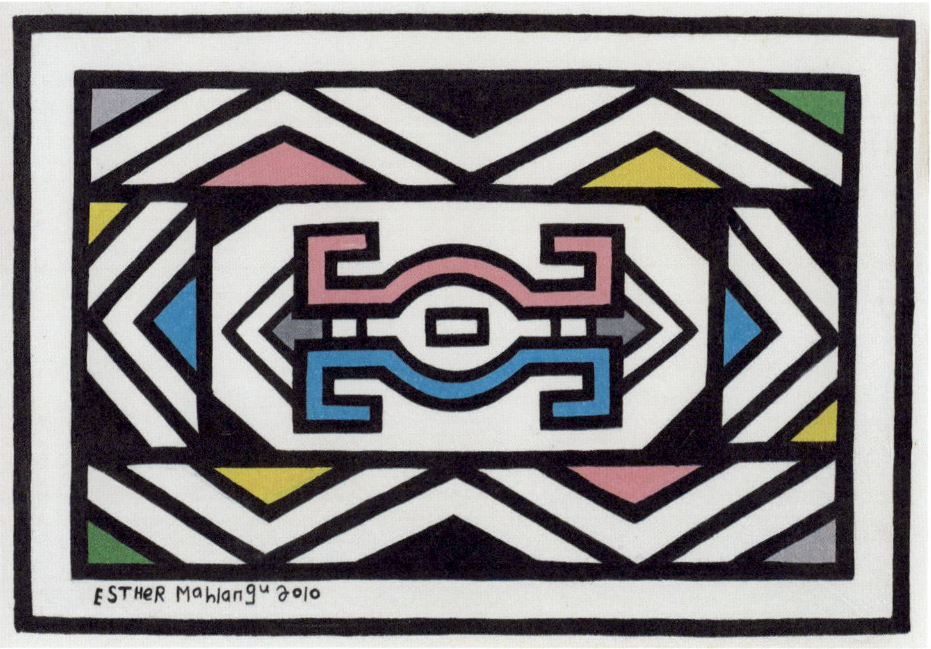
ESTHER Mahlangu 2010

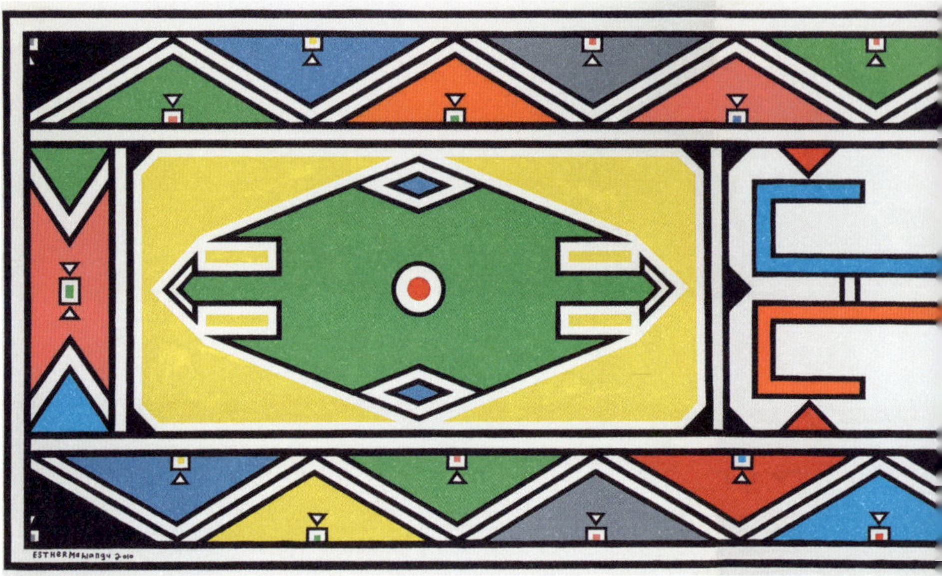
ESTHERMahlangu 2010

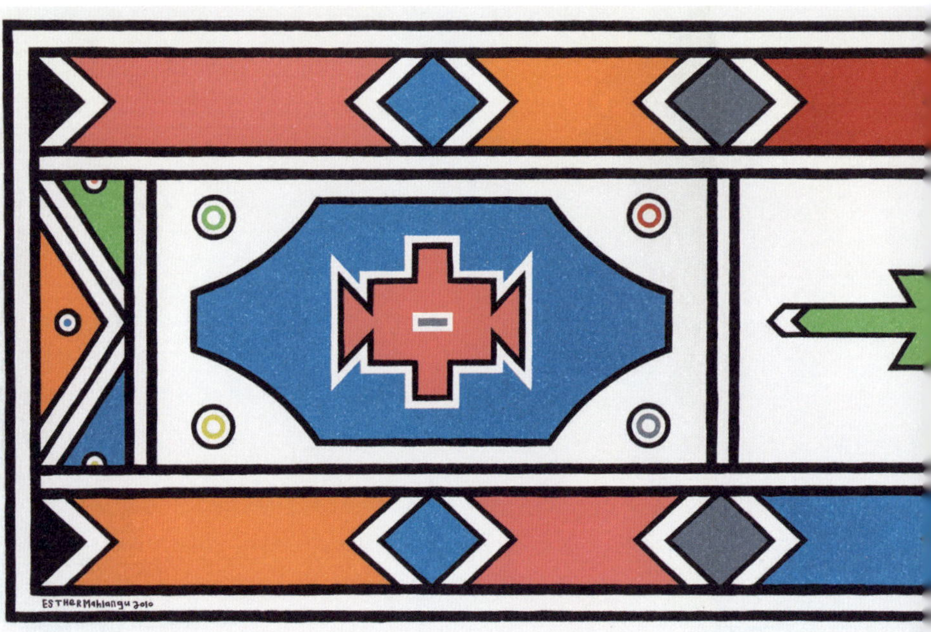
ESTHERMahlangu 2010

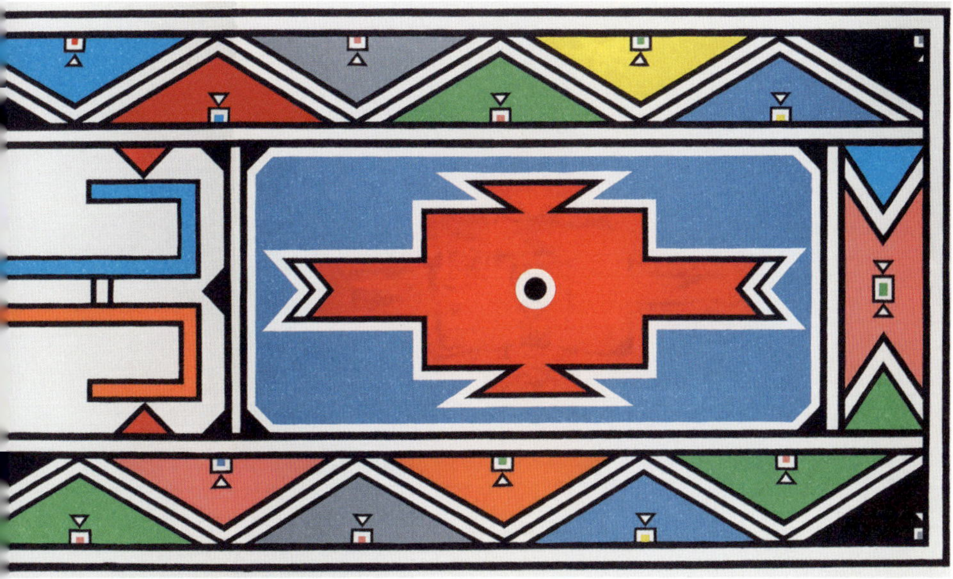

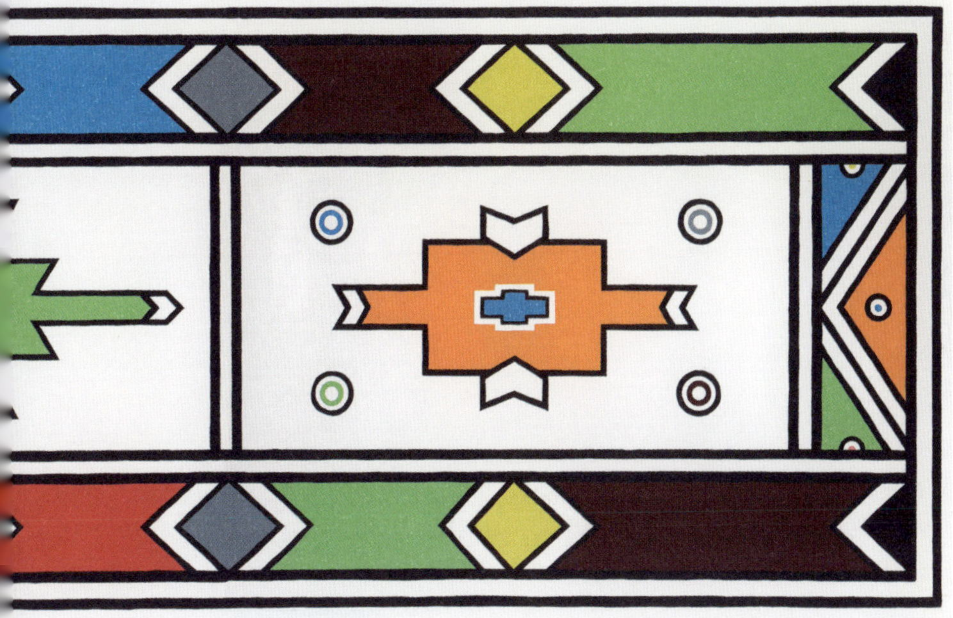

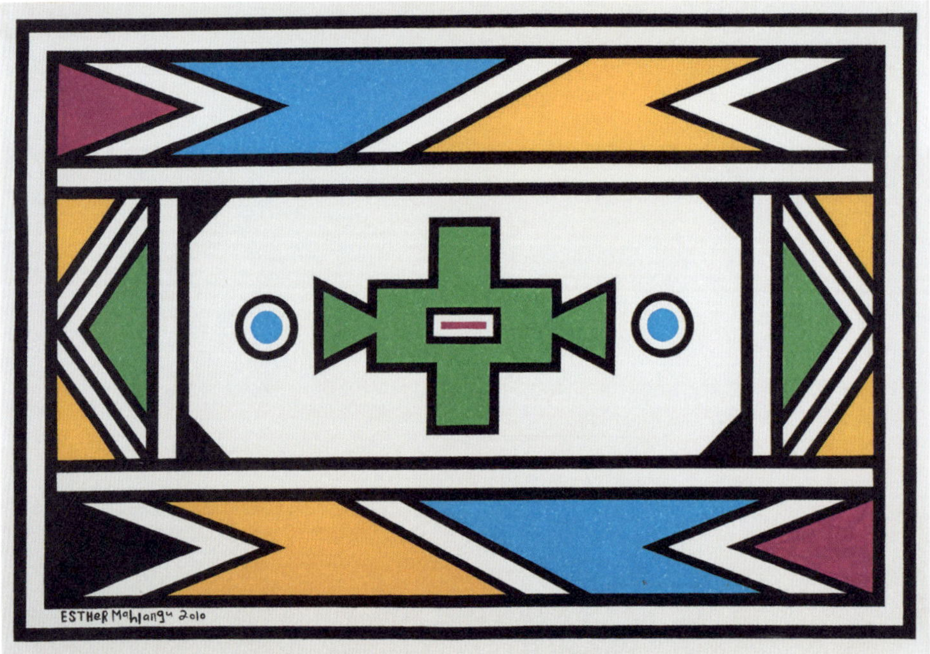
ESTHER Mahlangu 2010

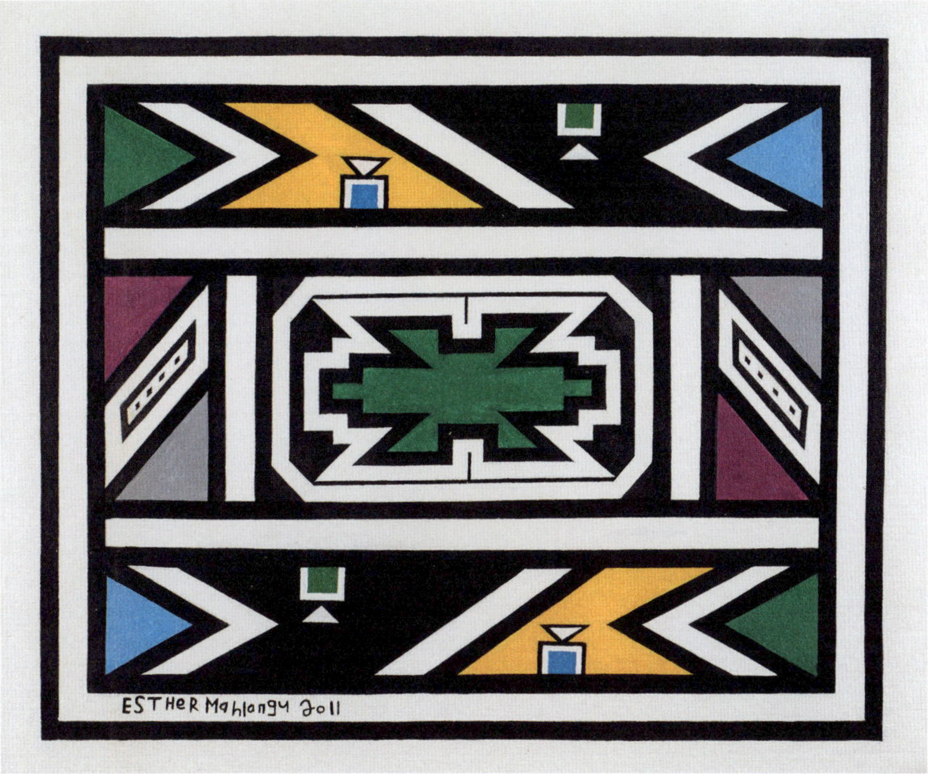
ESTHER Mahlangu 2011

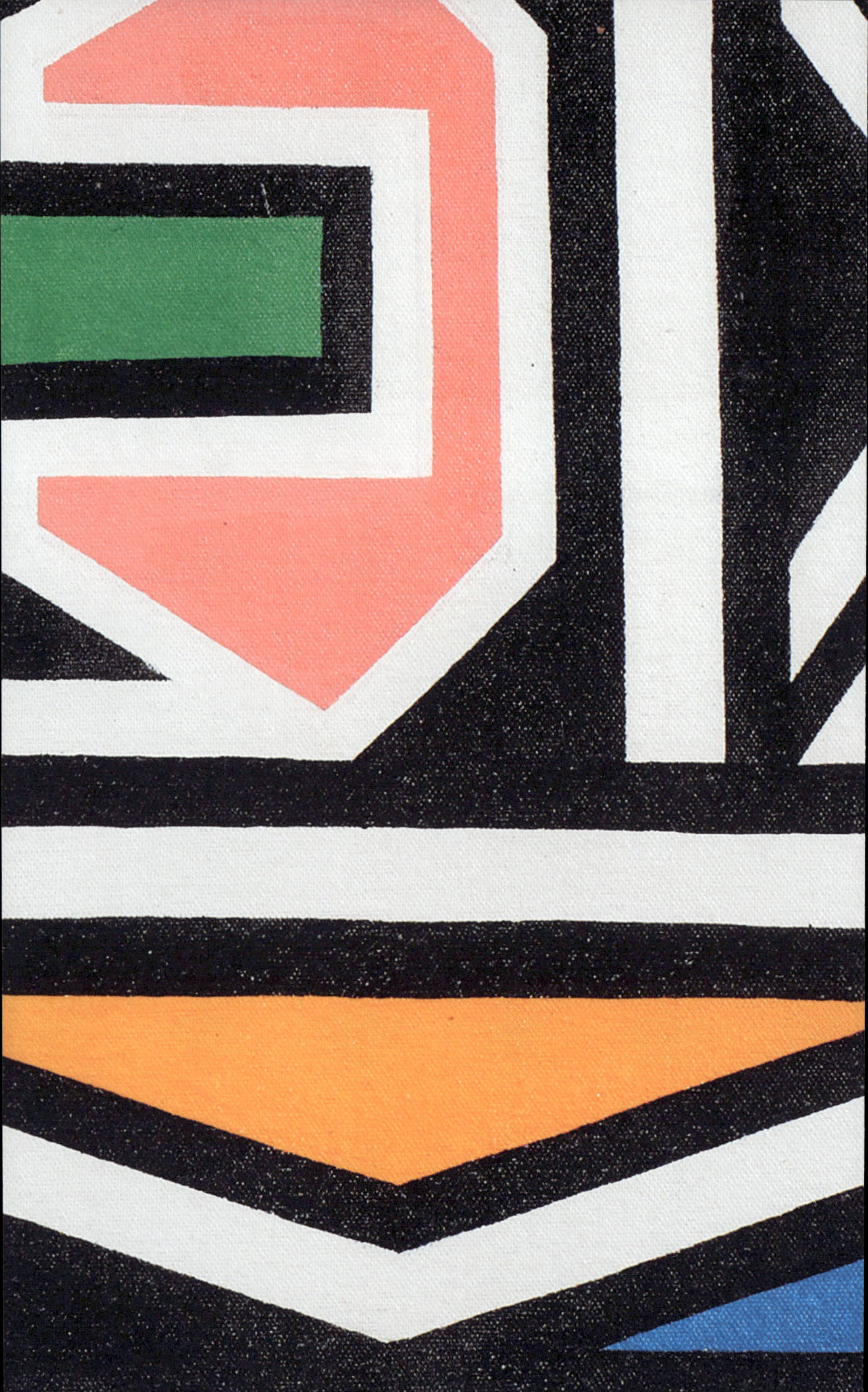

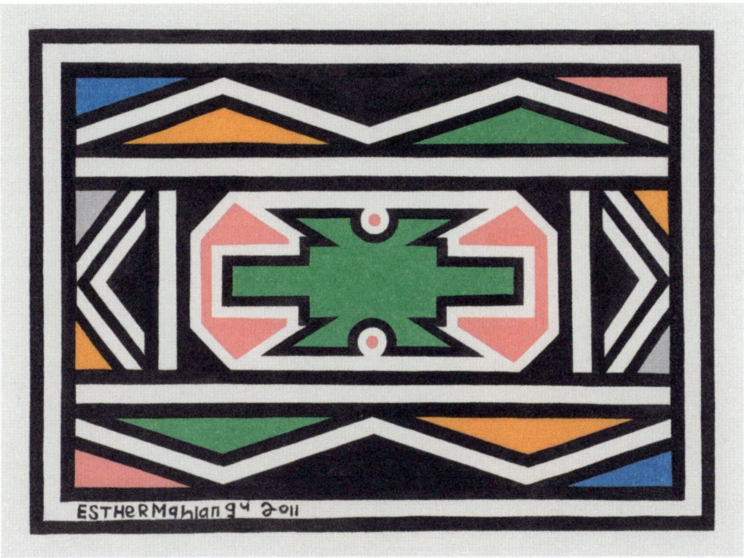

The old must change, otherwise it dies ... My art has evolved from a tribal tradition of decorating the home to where I am now.

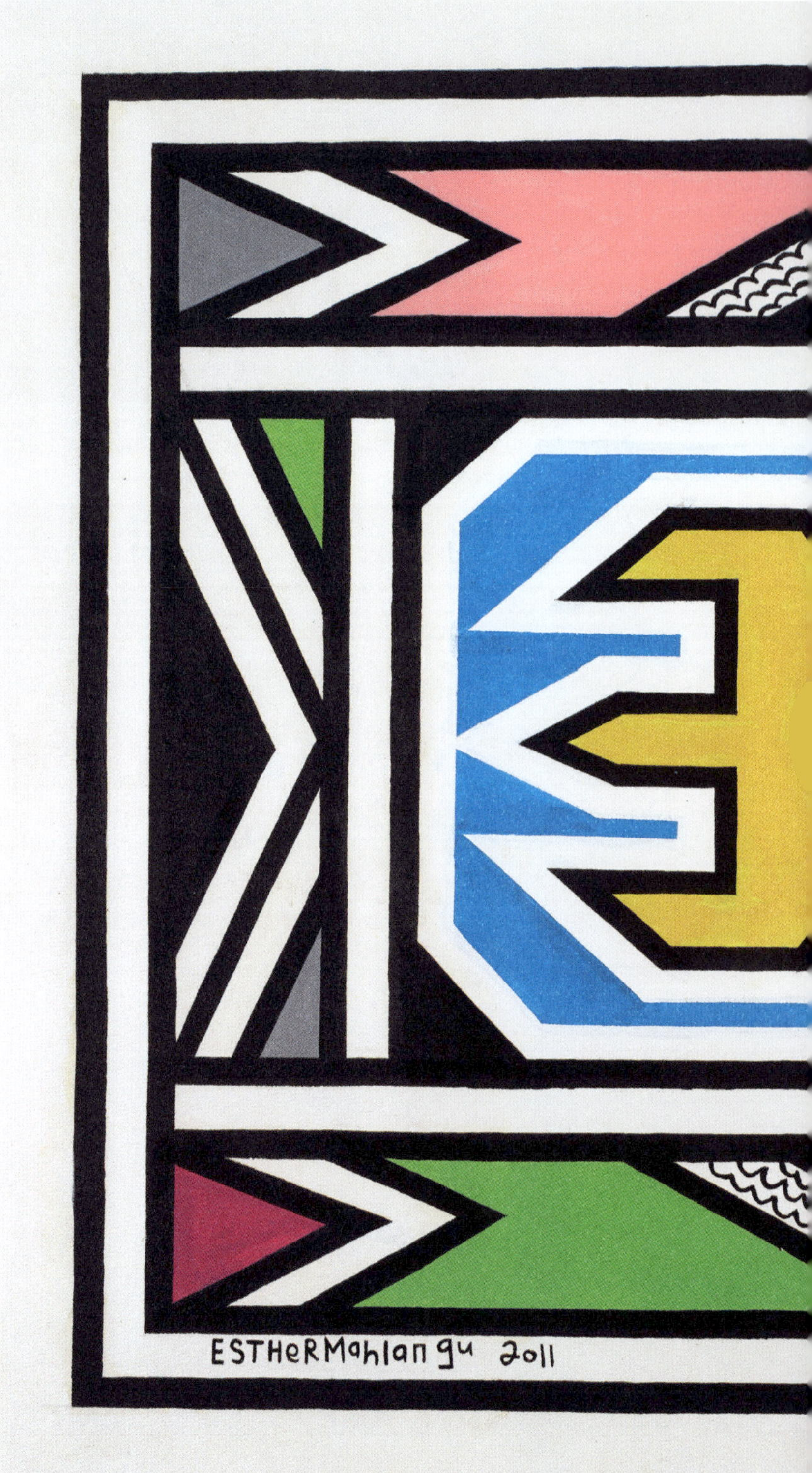
ESTHERMahlangu 2011

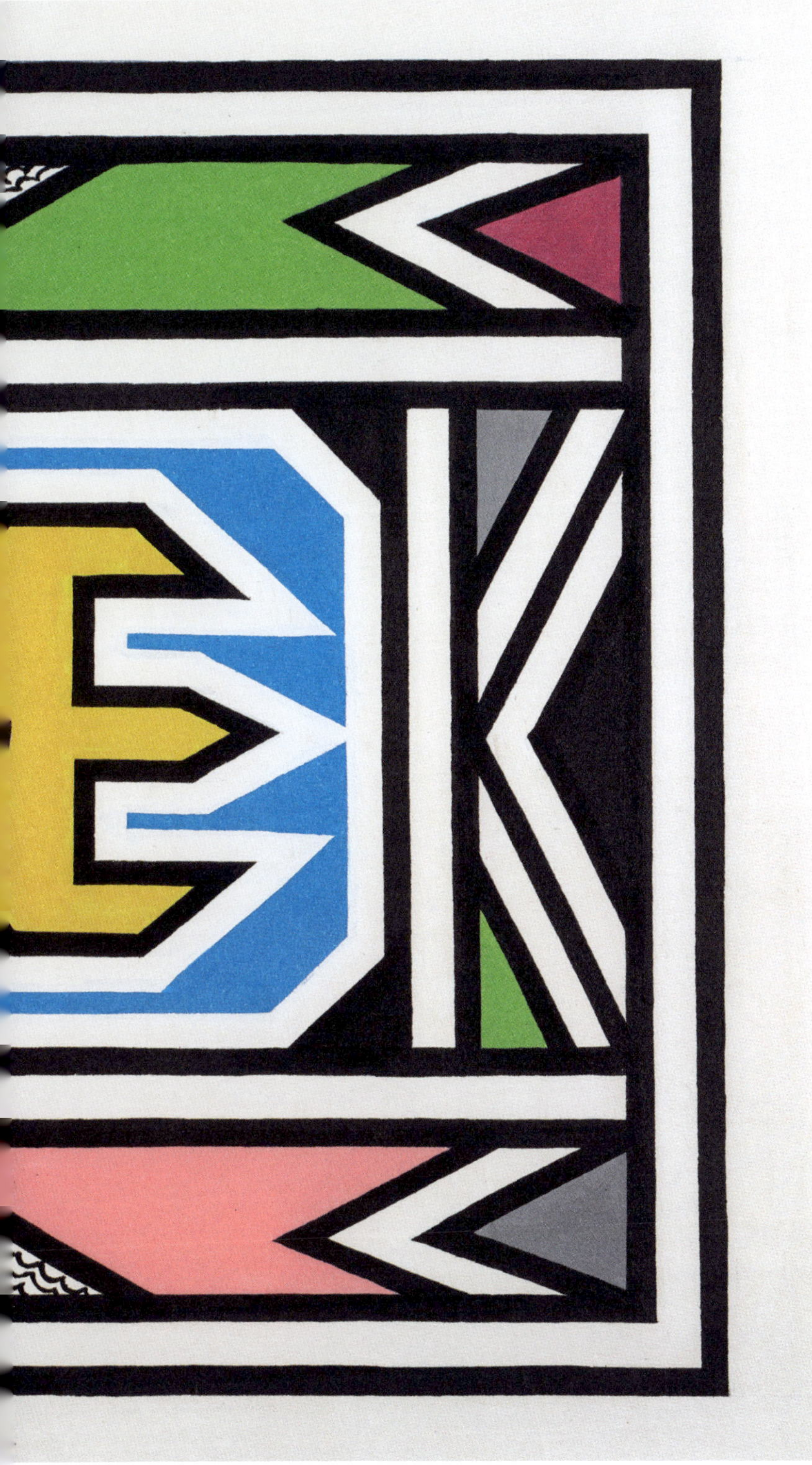

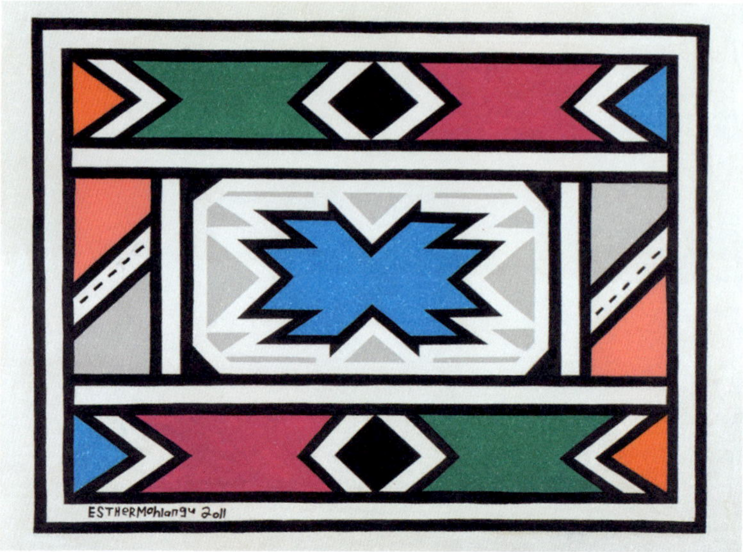
ESTHERMahlangu 2011

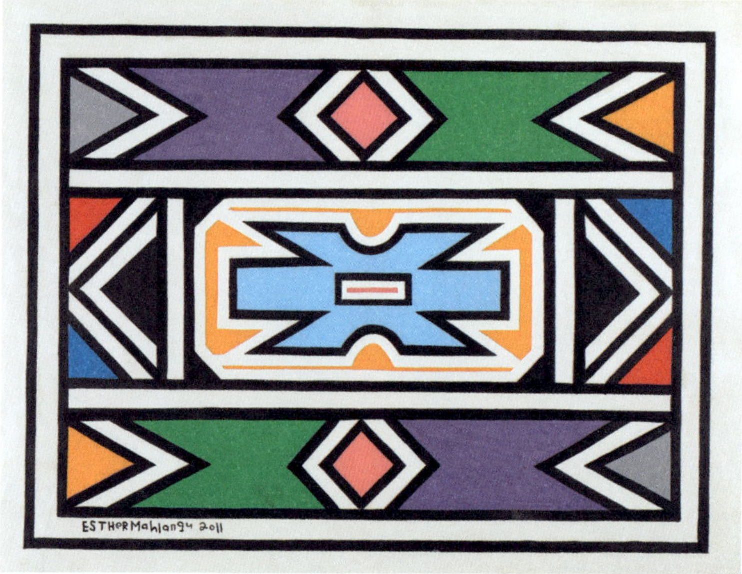
ESTHERMahlangu 2011

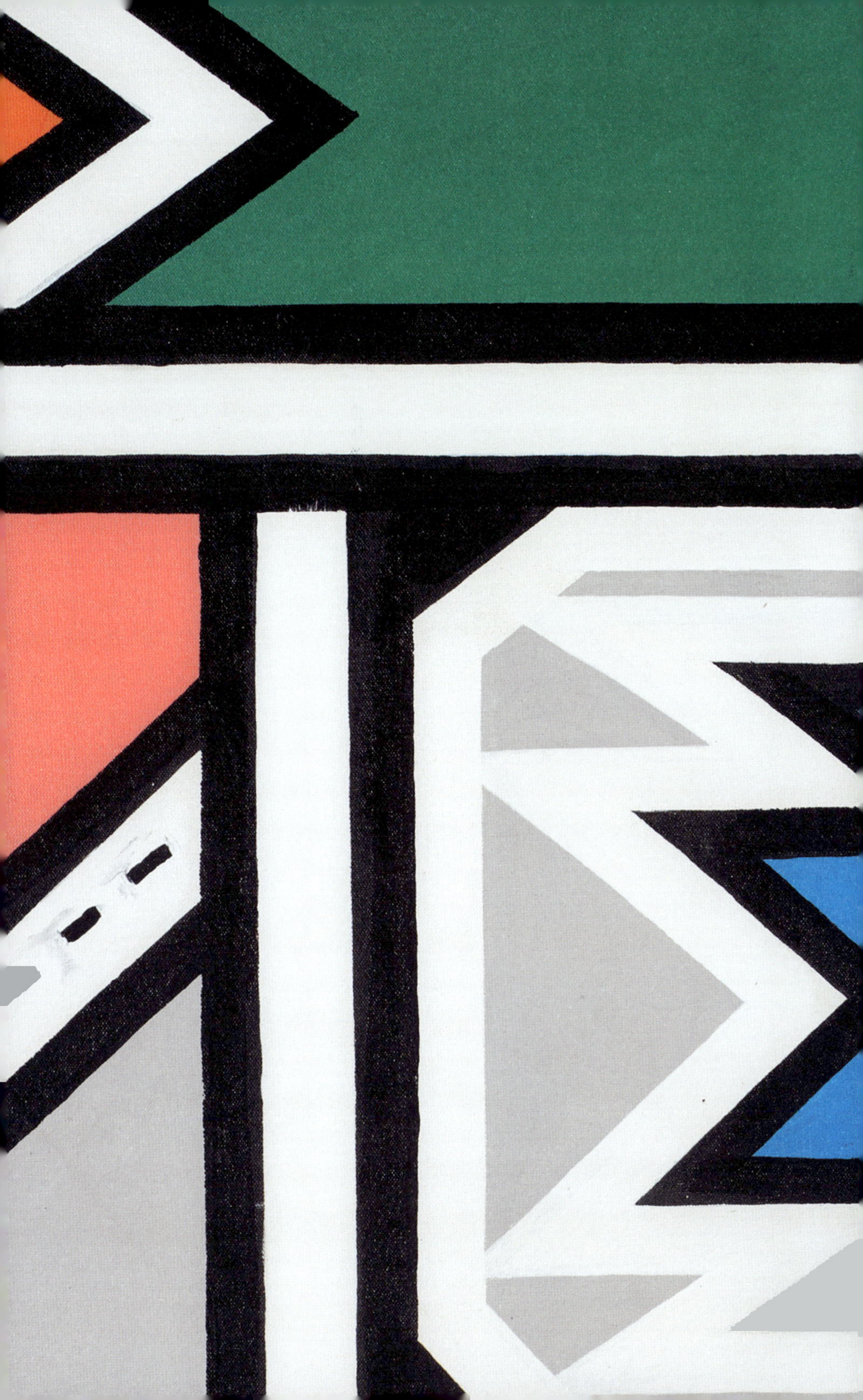

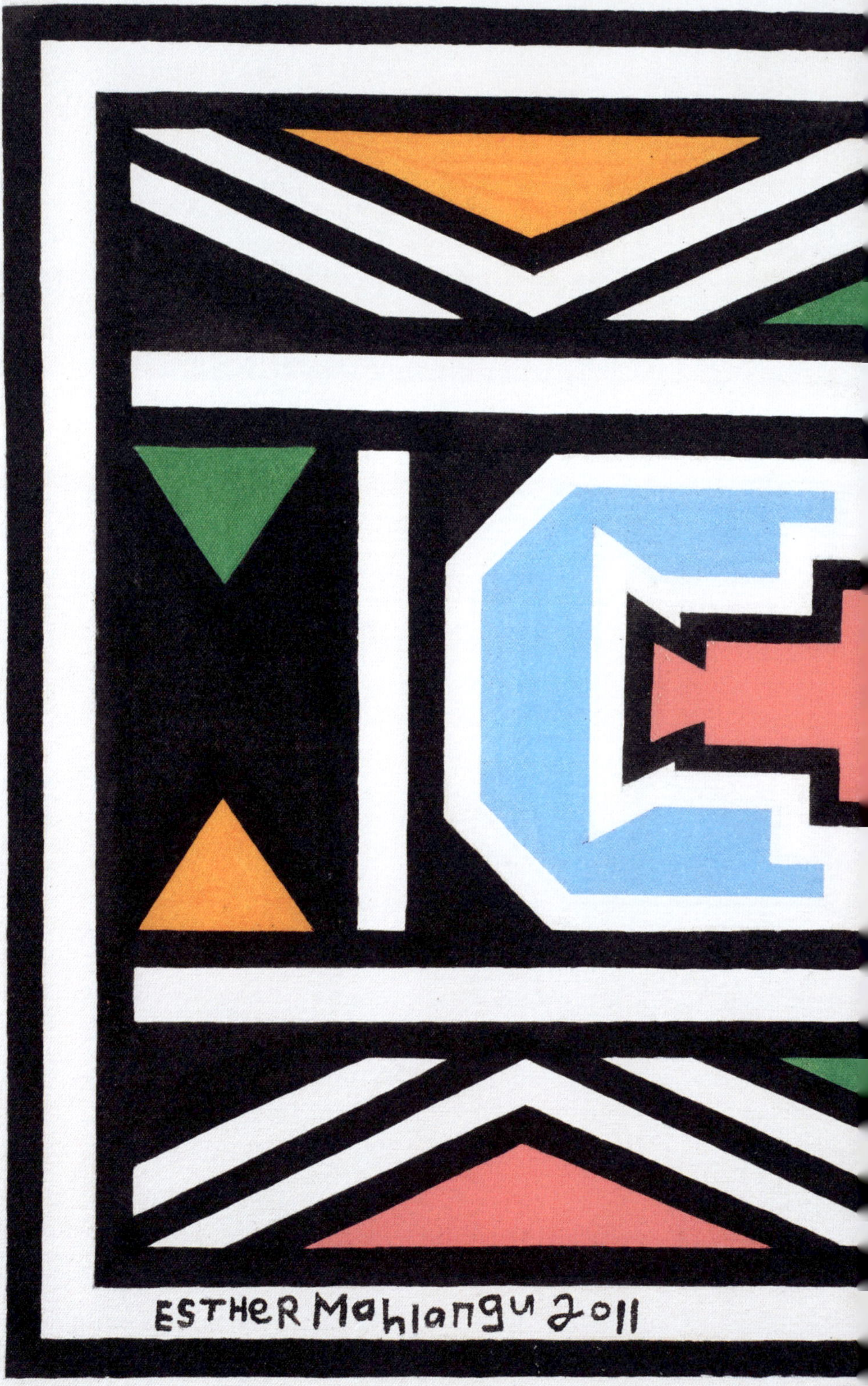
ESTHER Mahlangu 2011

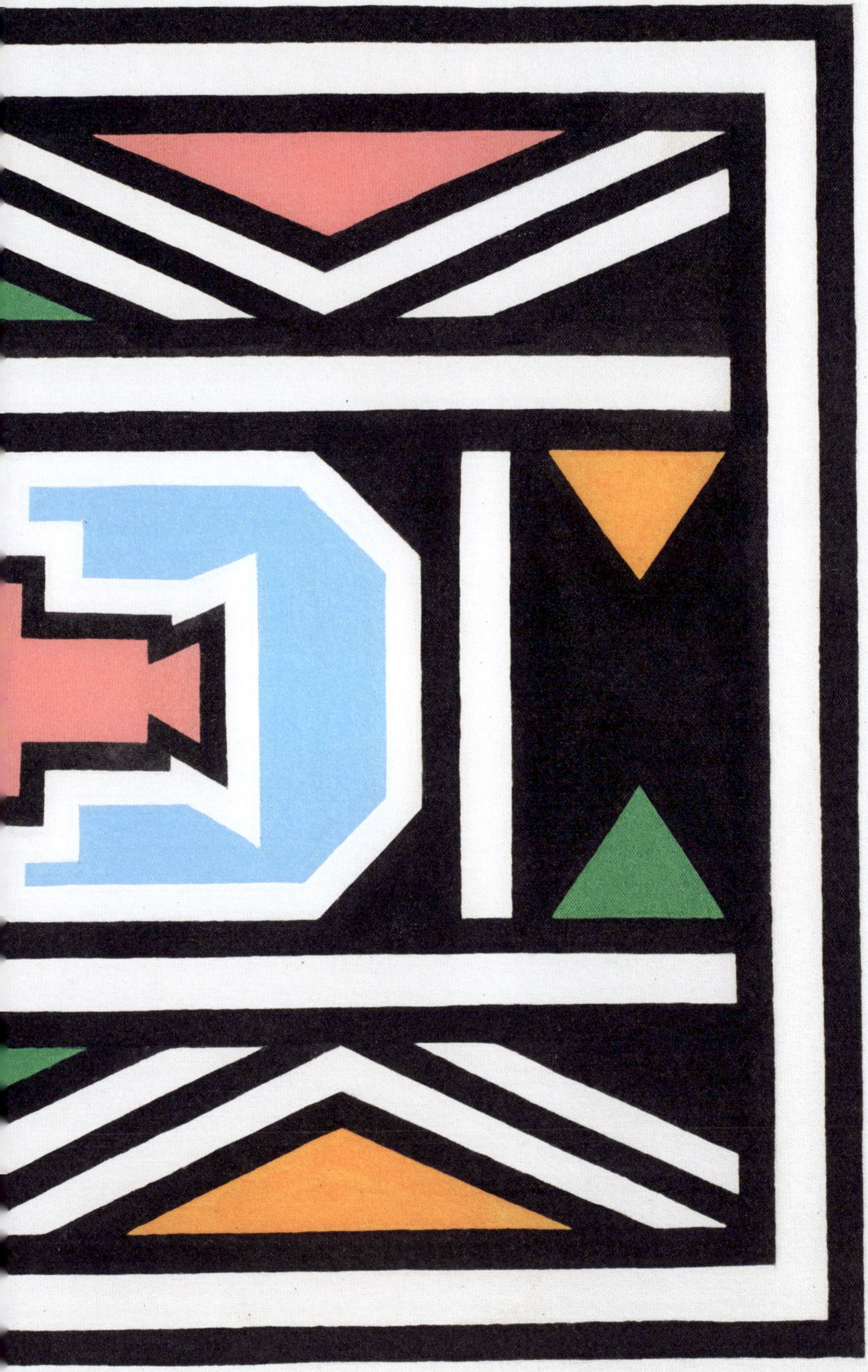

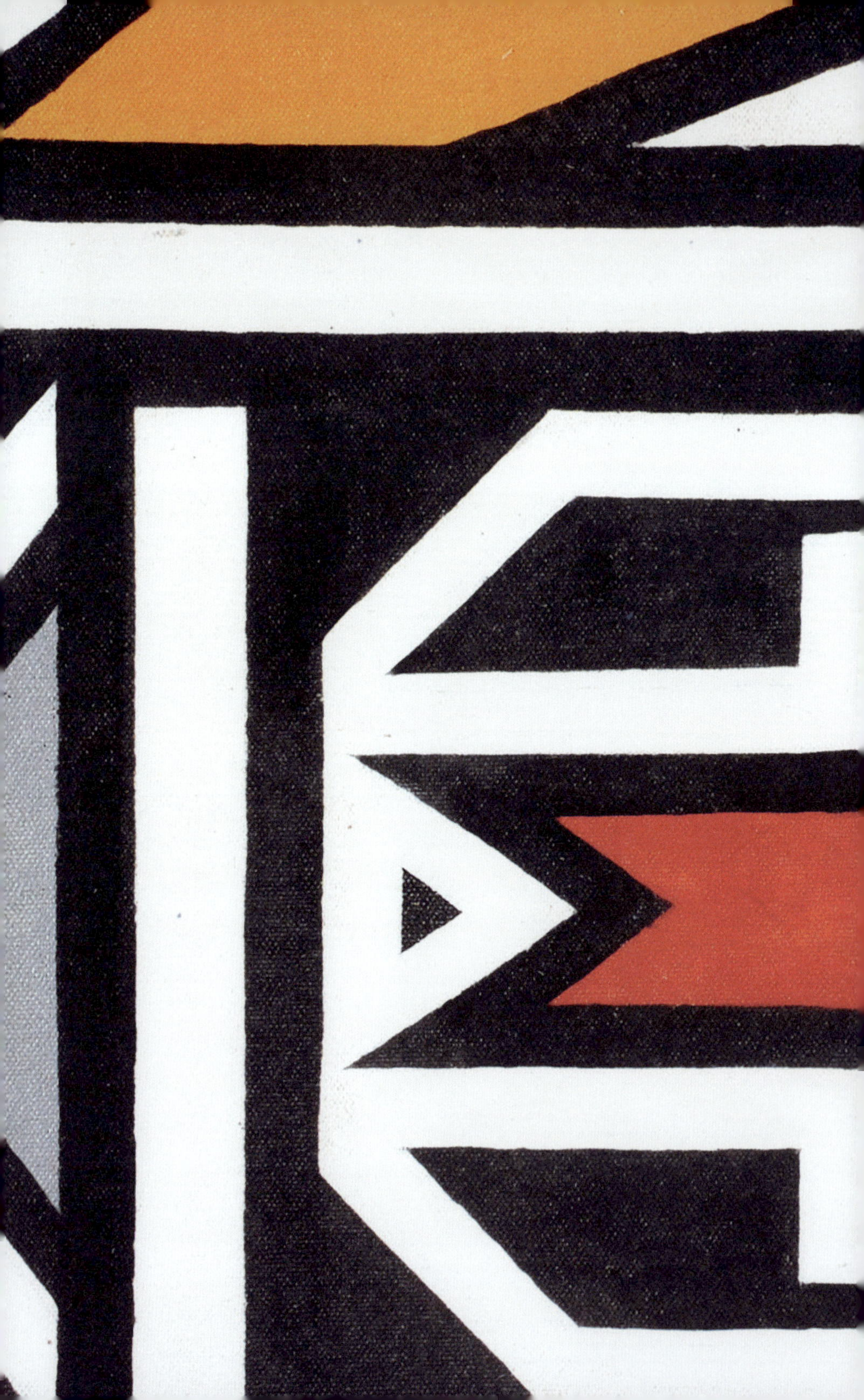

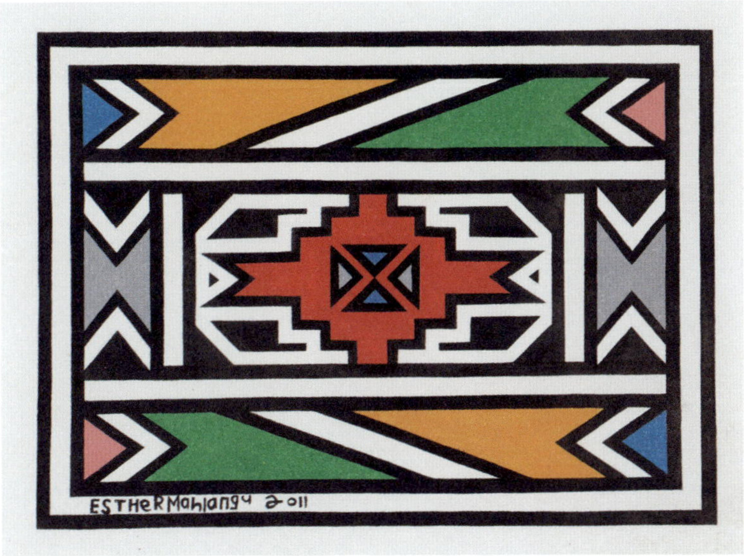

Ndebele art has shown me the world
and people overseas love it.

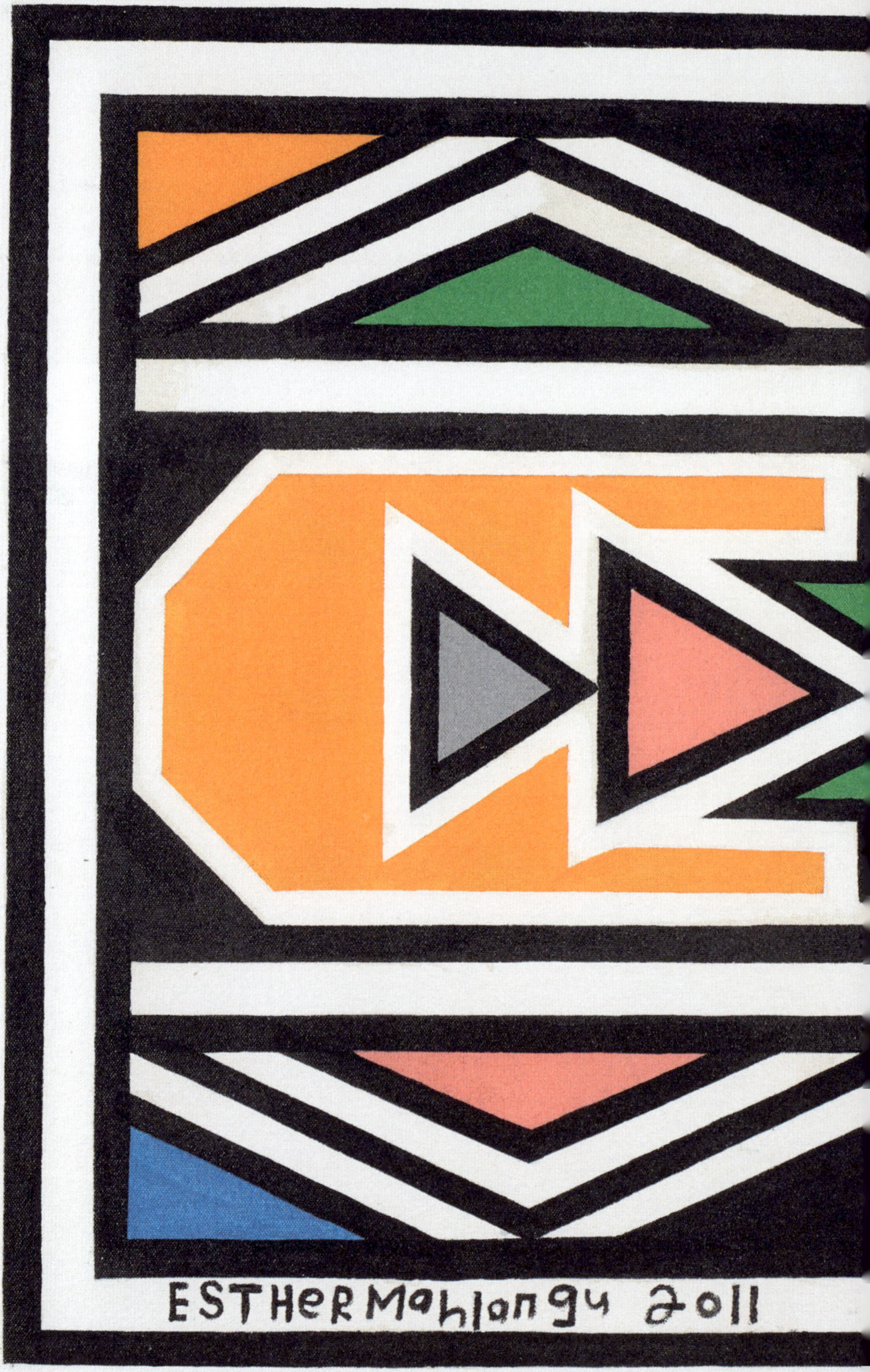
ESTHER Mahlangu 2011

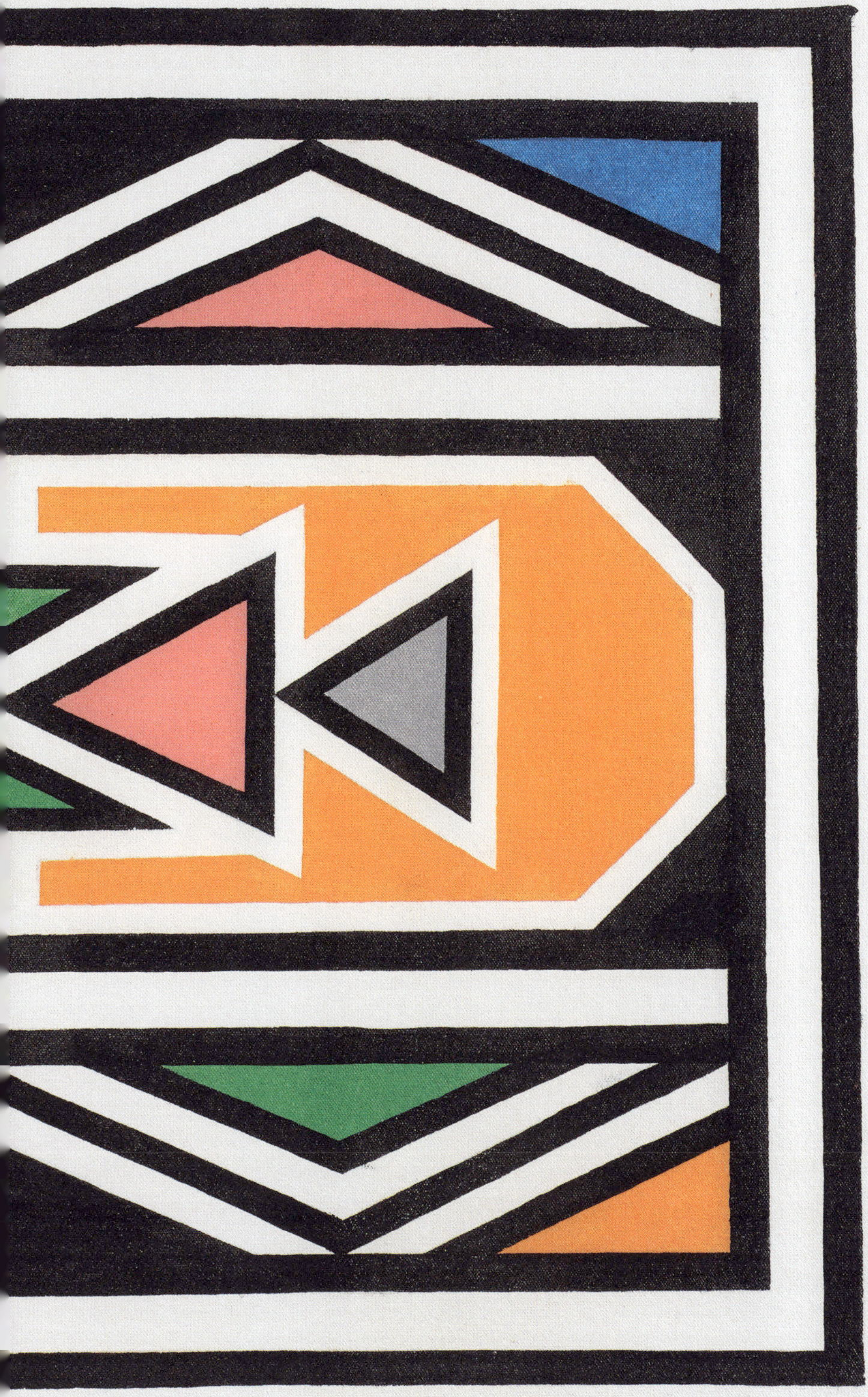

The original patterns that were painted on the houses in the past, were ... used to announce events like births and deaths, and even weddings.

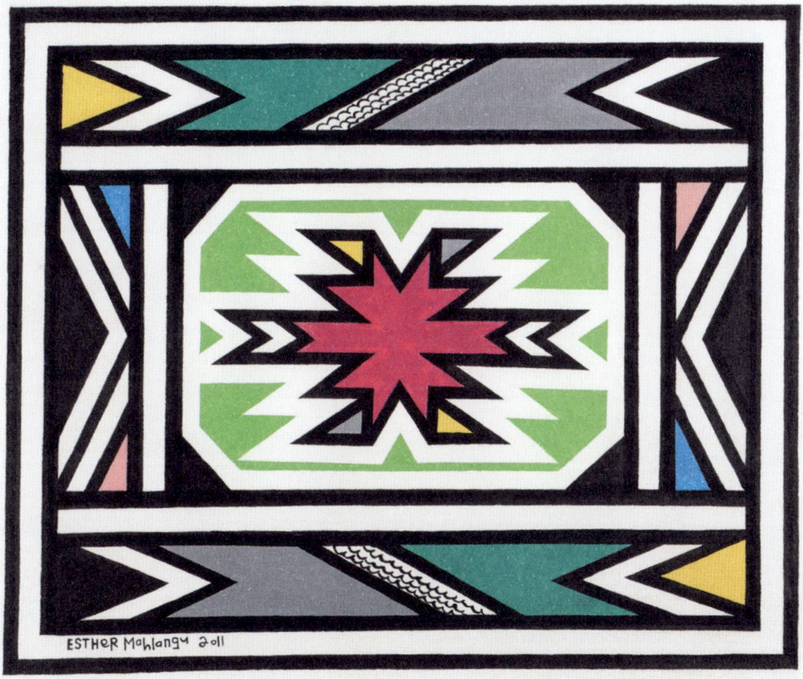
ESTHER Mahlangu 2011

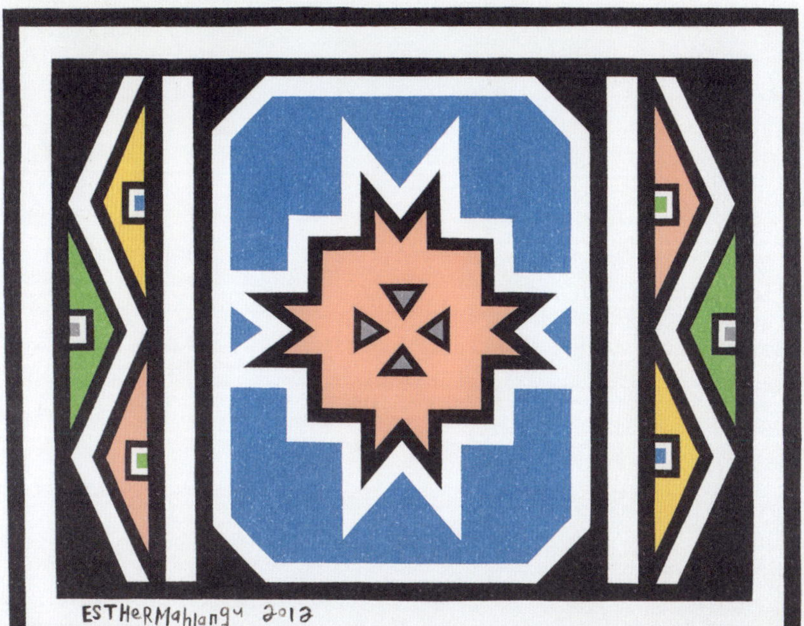
ESTHERMahlangu 2012

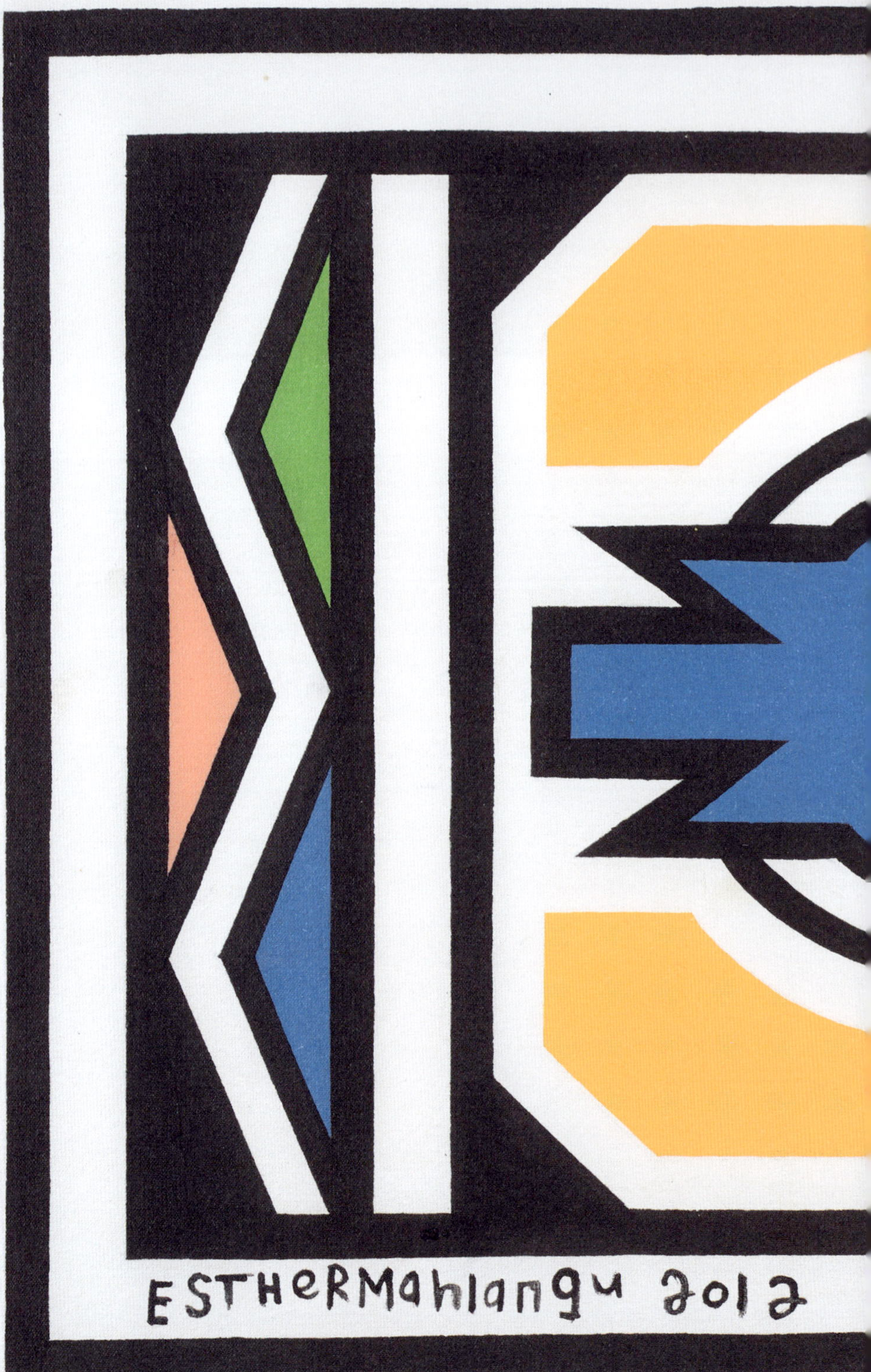
ESTHERMahlangu 2012

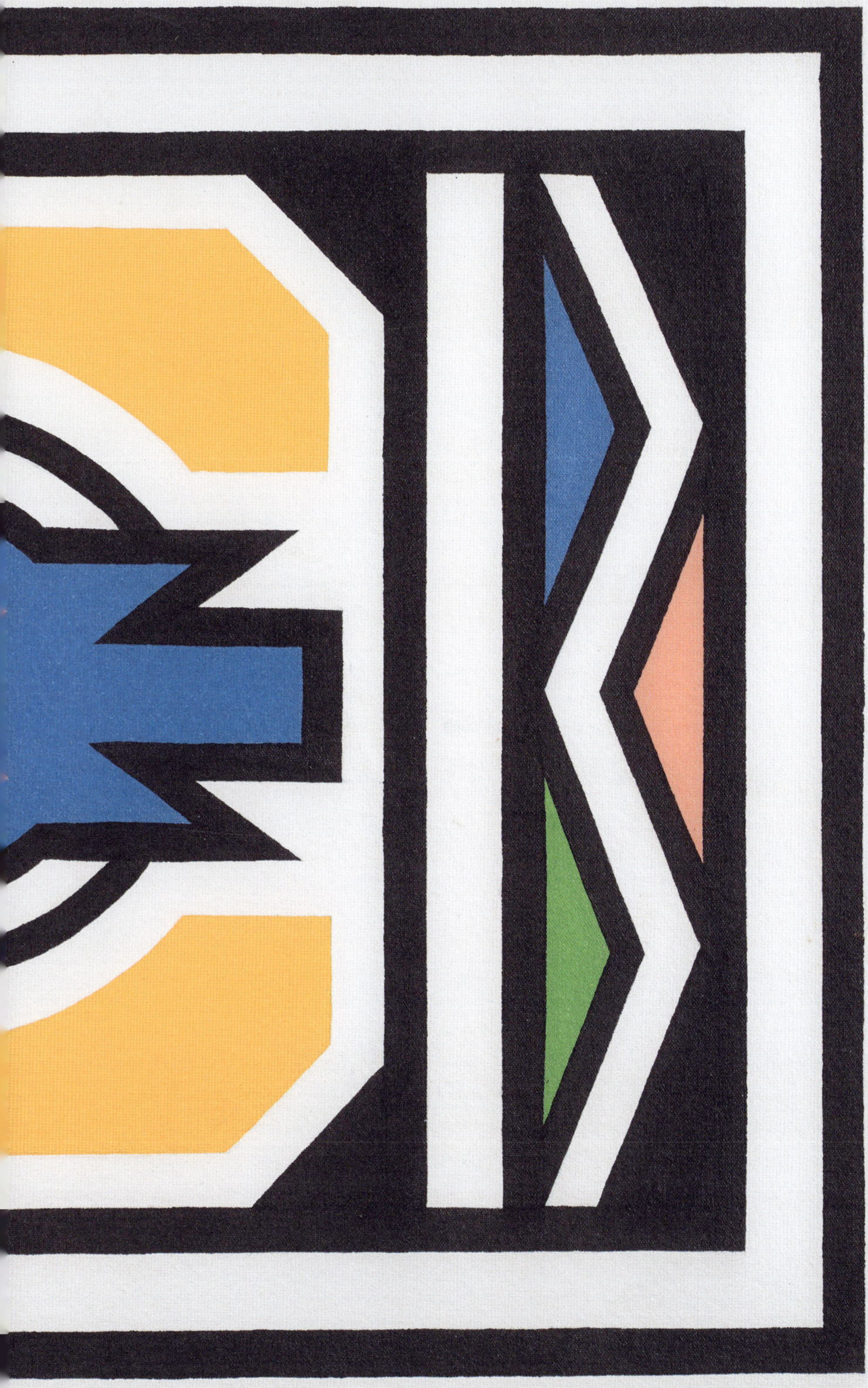

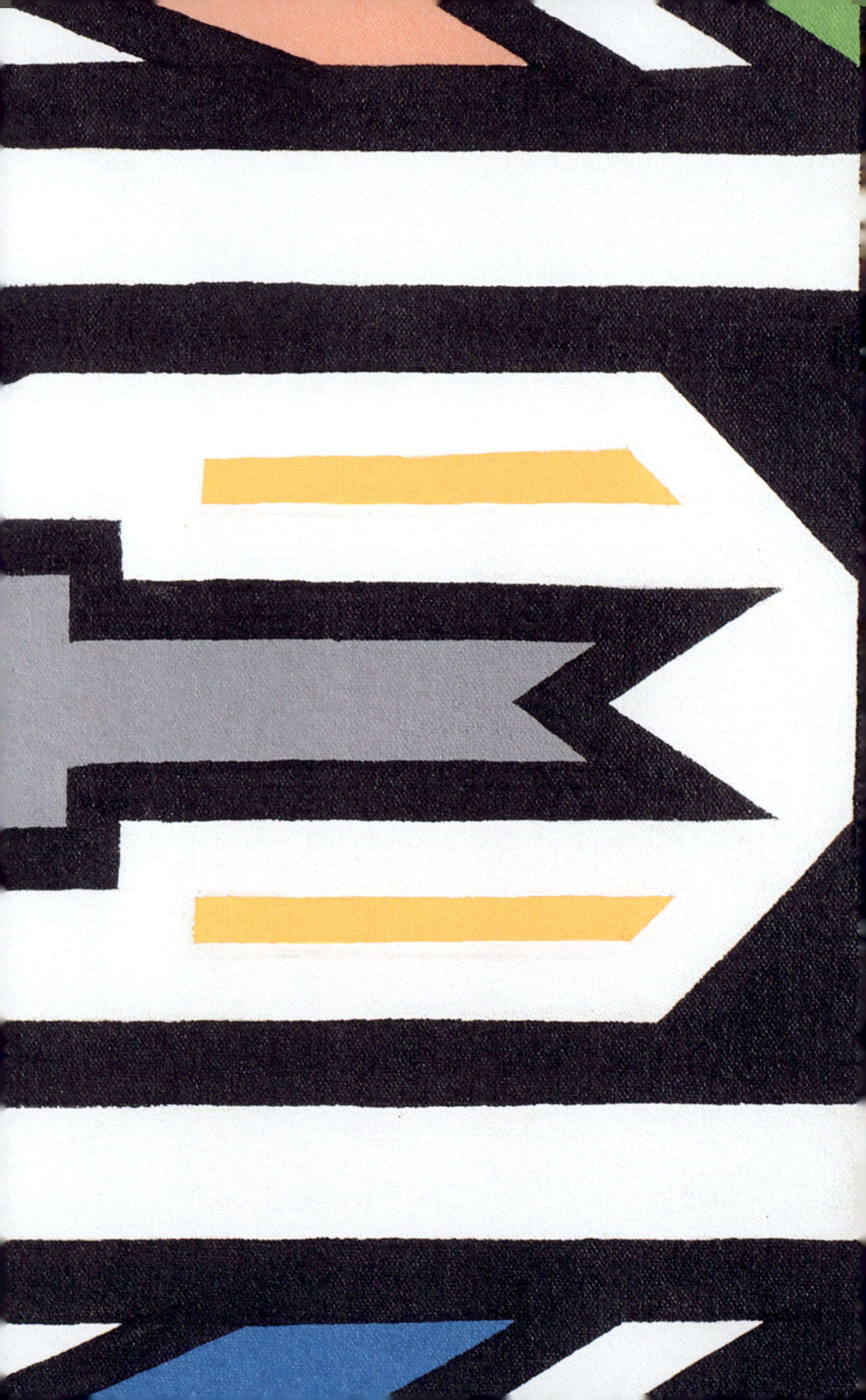

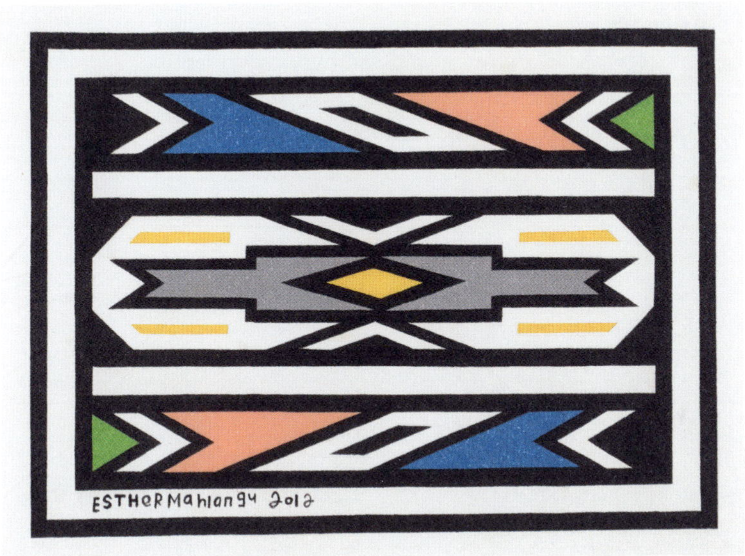

I sometimes combine the old
and the new ... As I was exposed
to the new modern colours
and paints, I adapted my motifs.
I built up a new vocabulary.

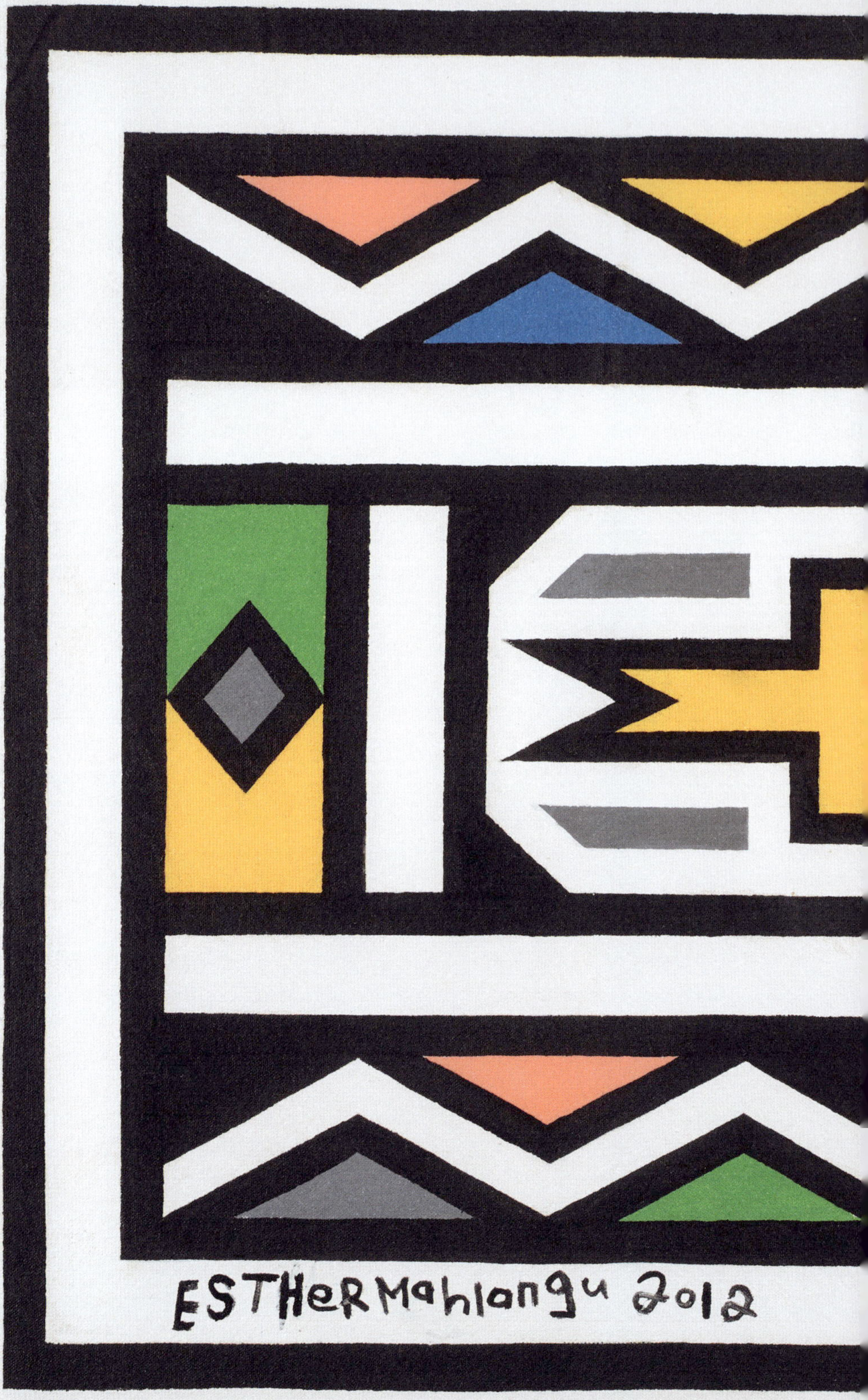
ESTHER Mahlangu 2012

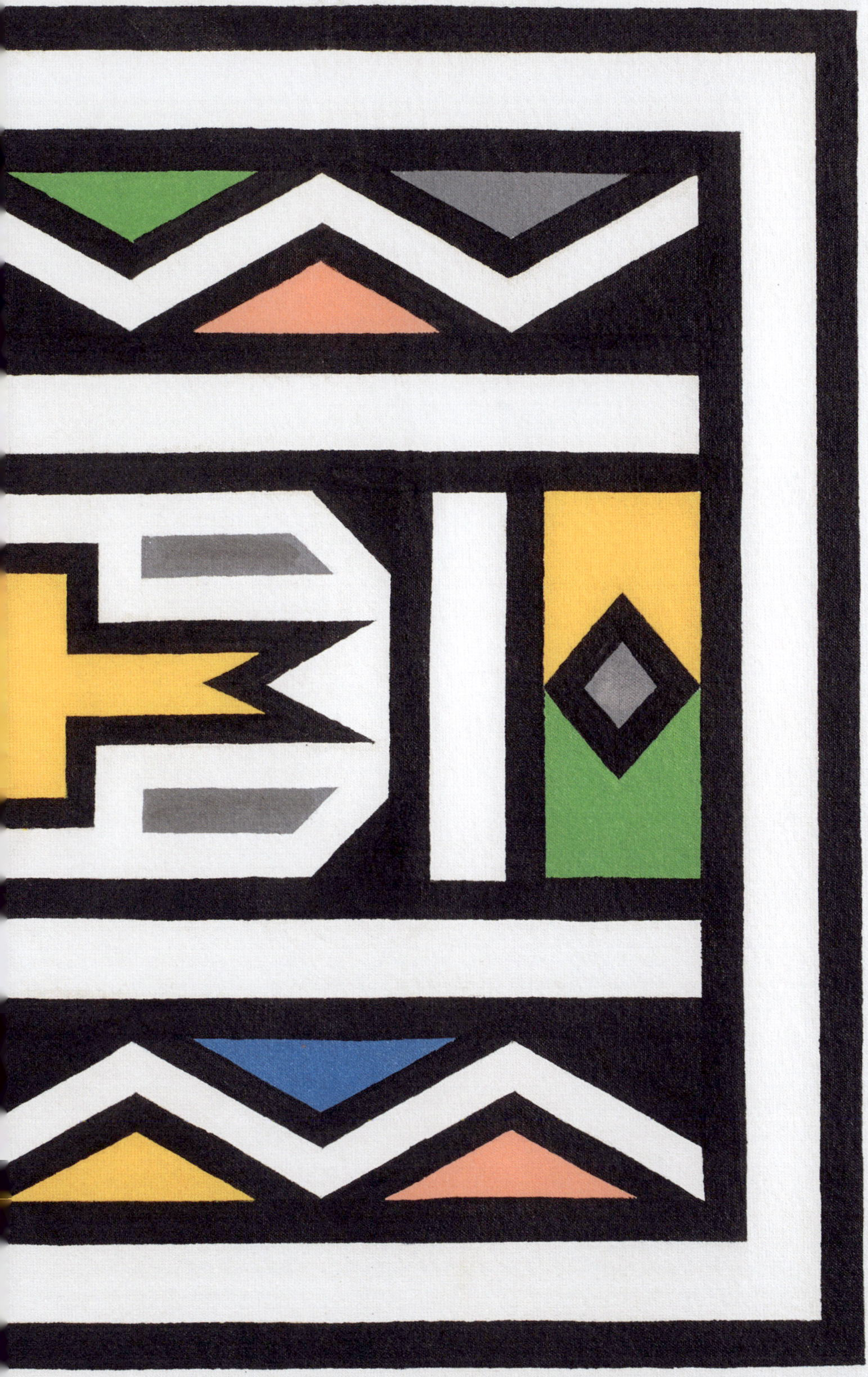

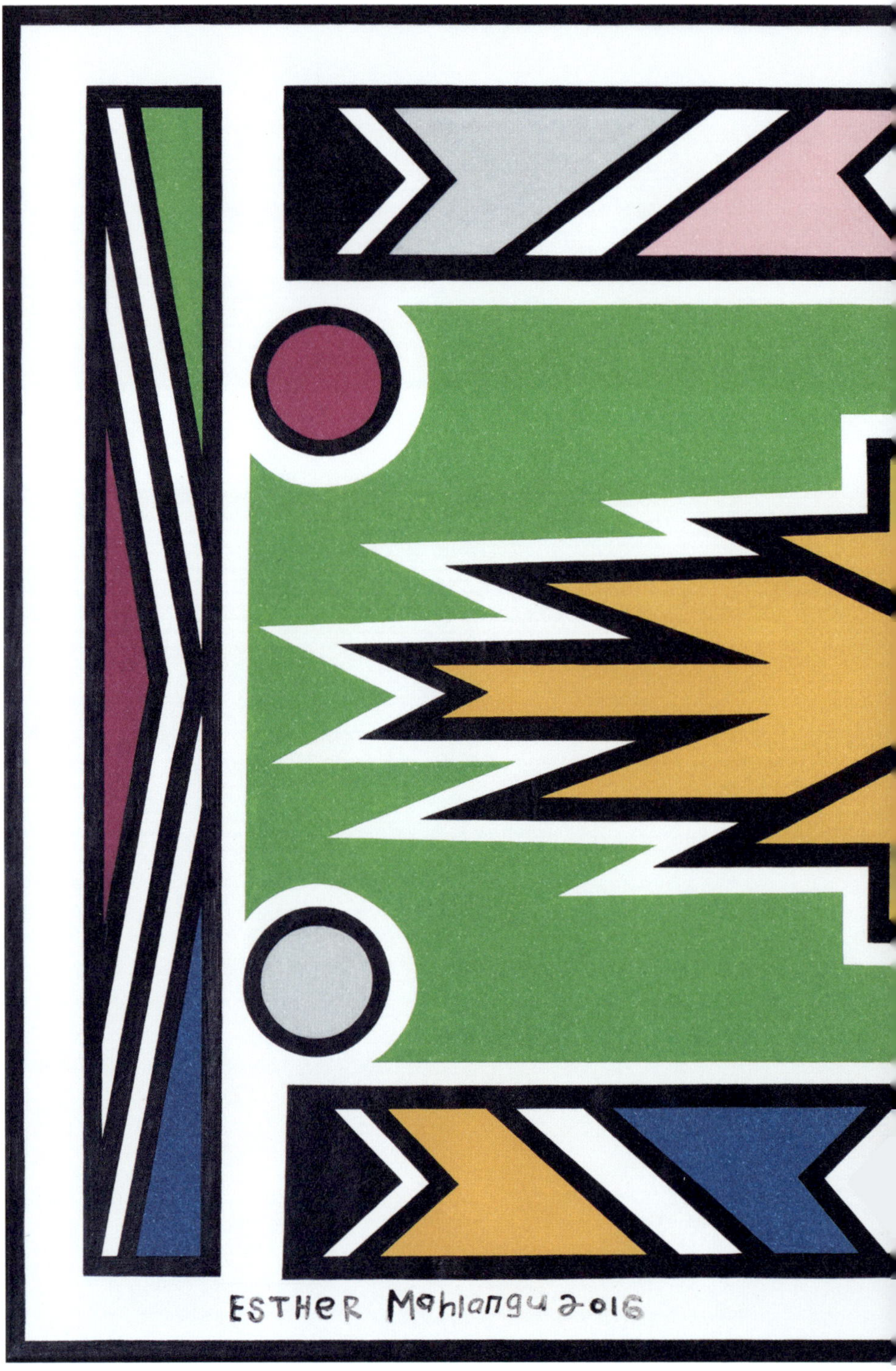
ESTHER Mahlangu 2016

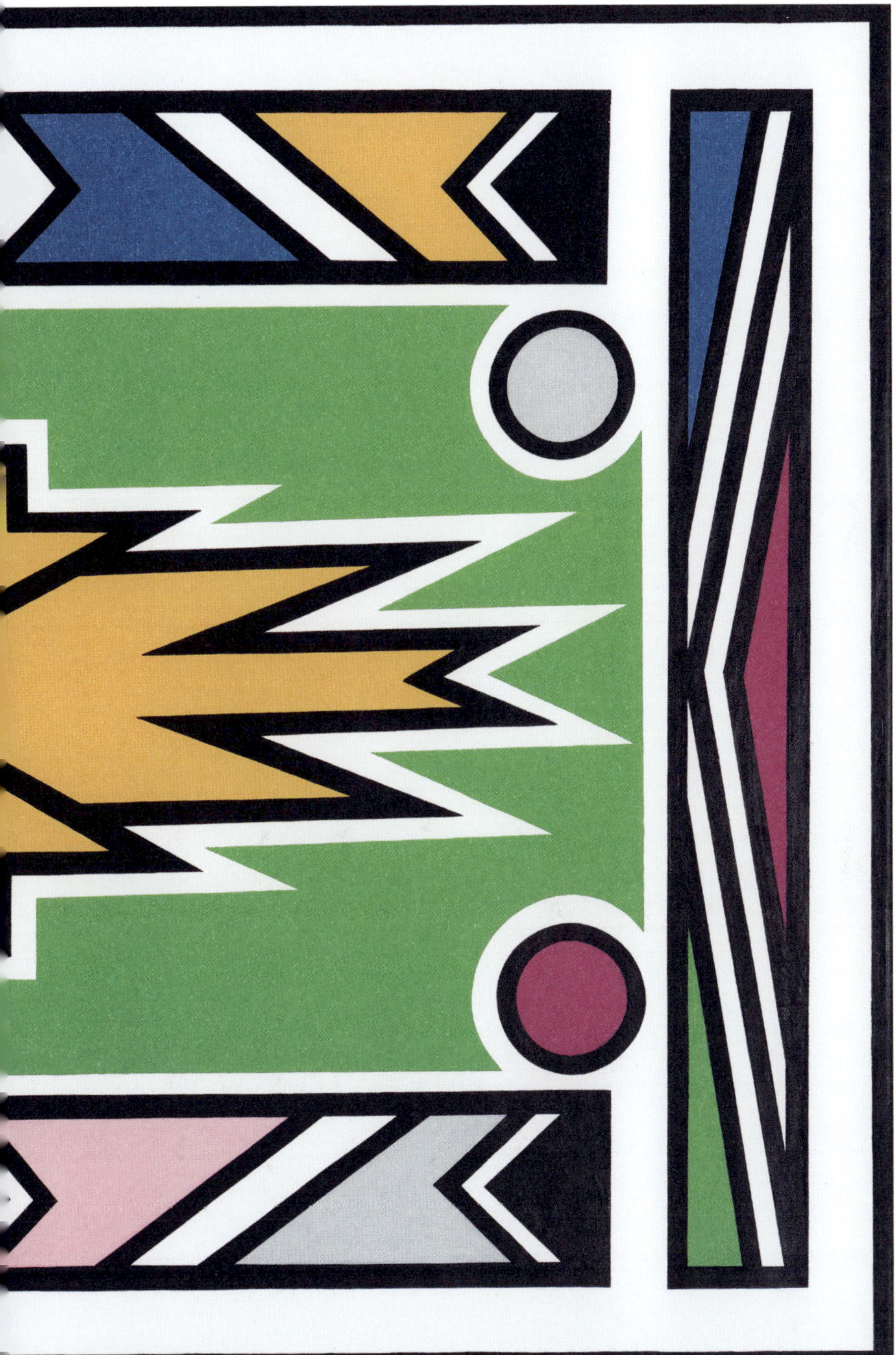

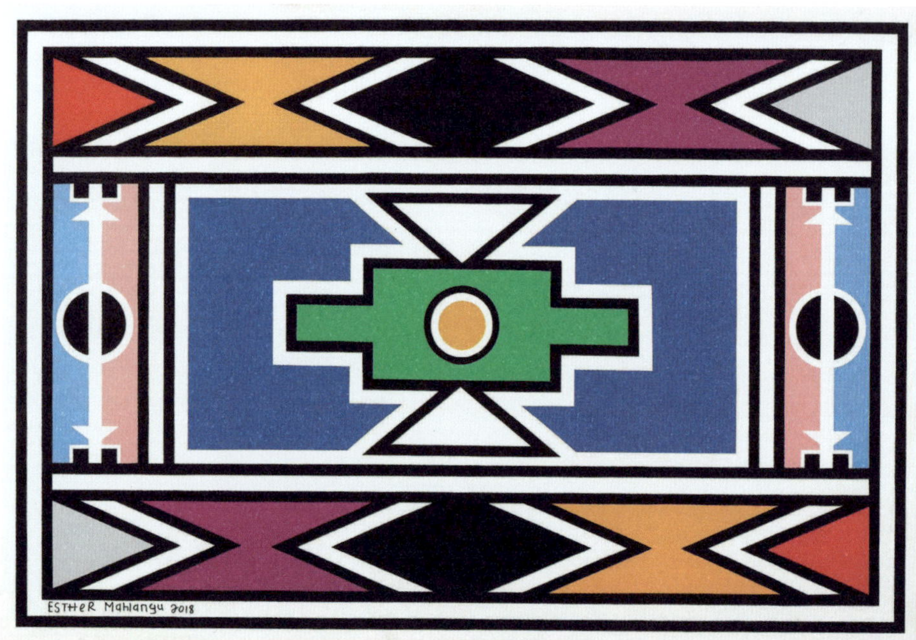
ESTHER Mahlangu 2018

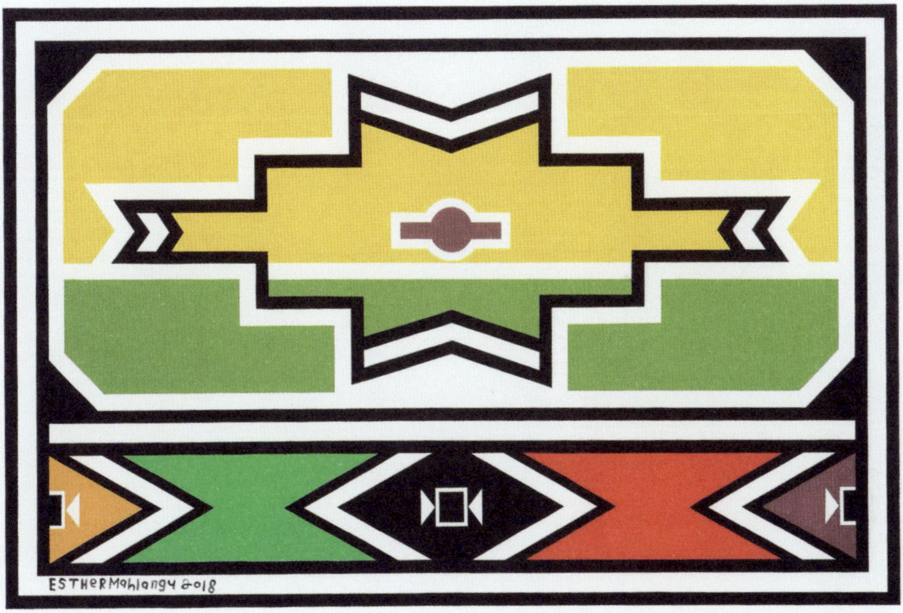
ESTHER Mahlangu 2018

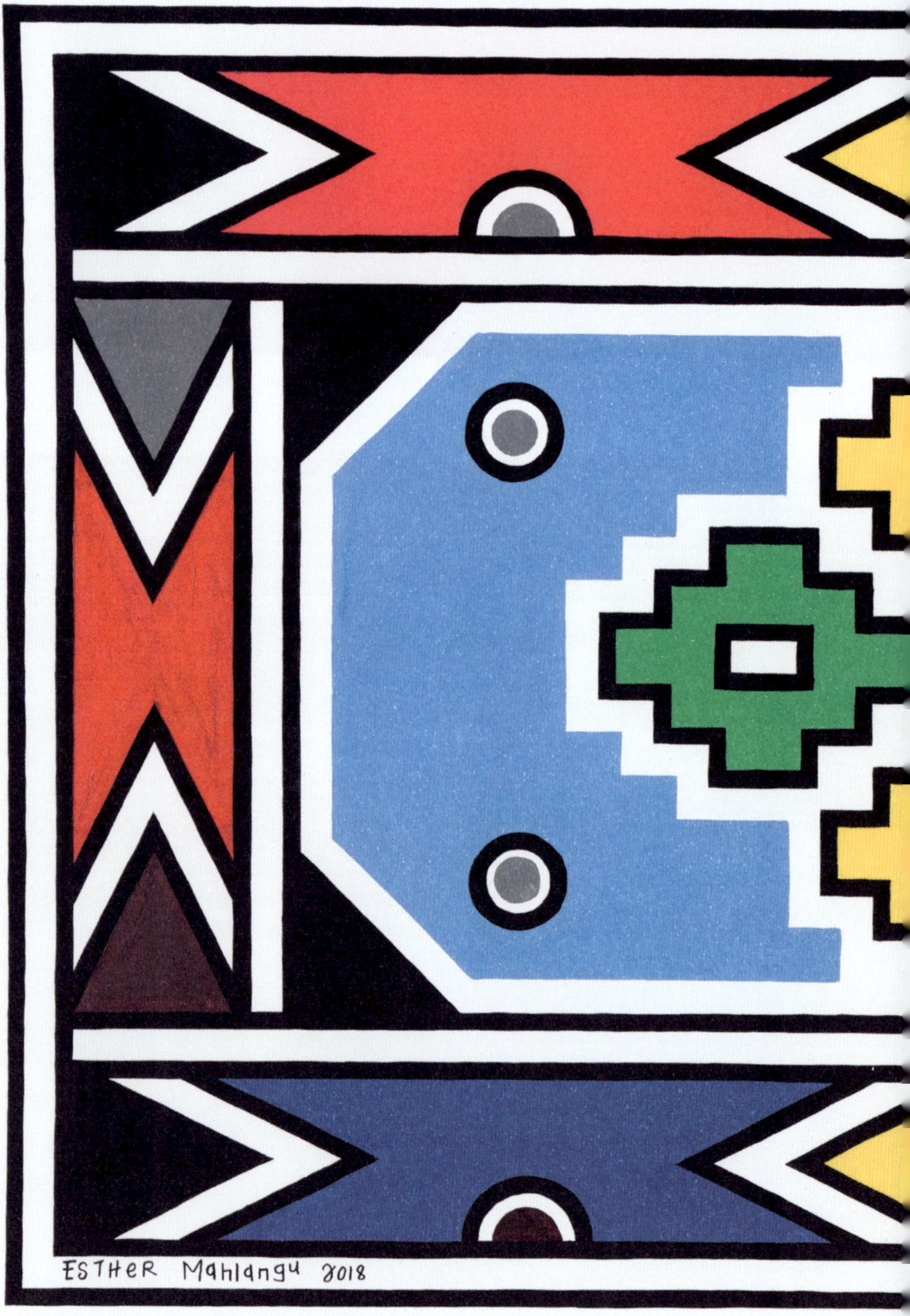
ESTHER Mahlangu 2018

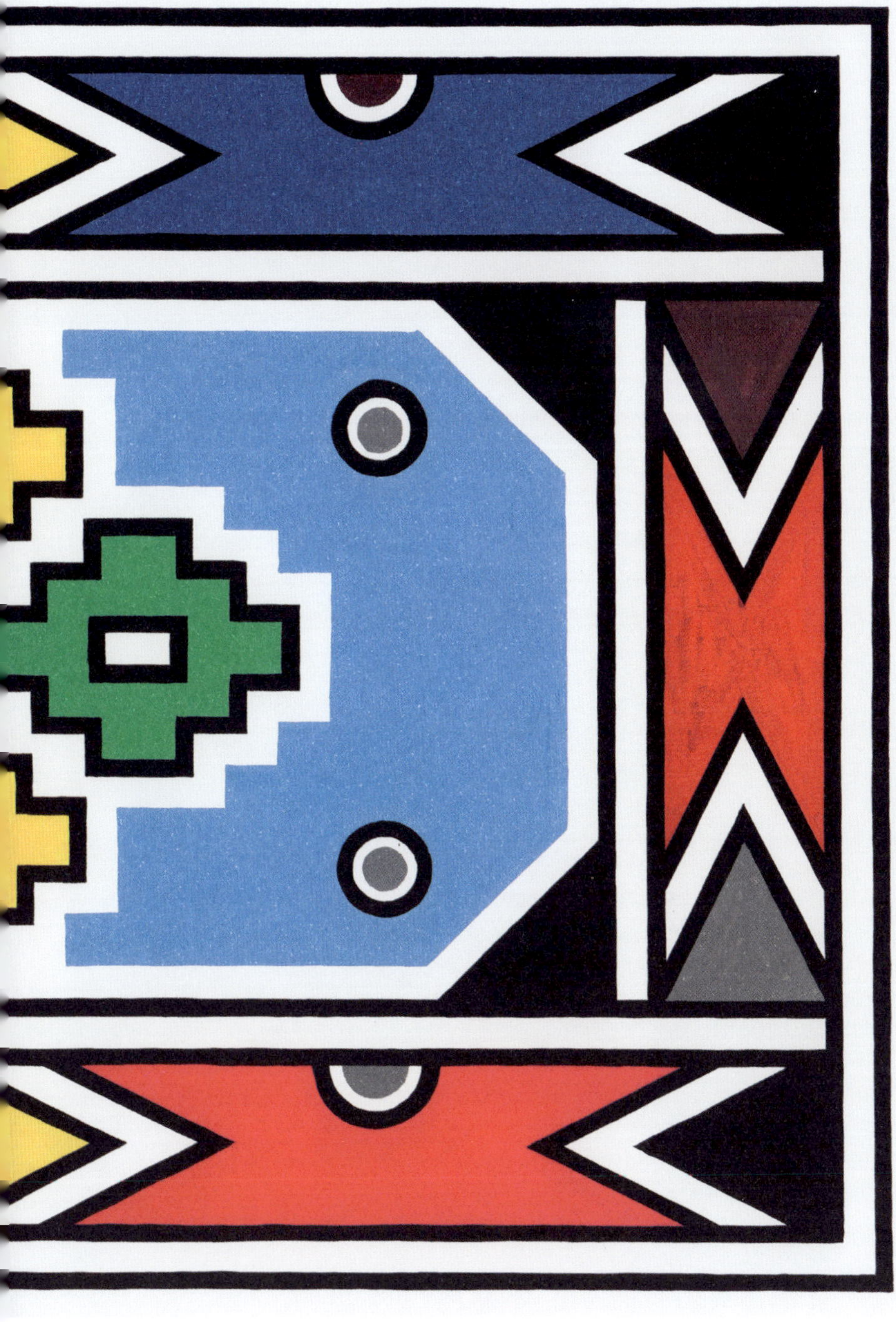

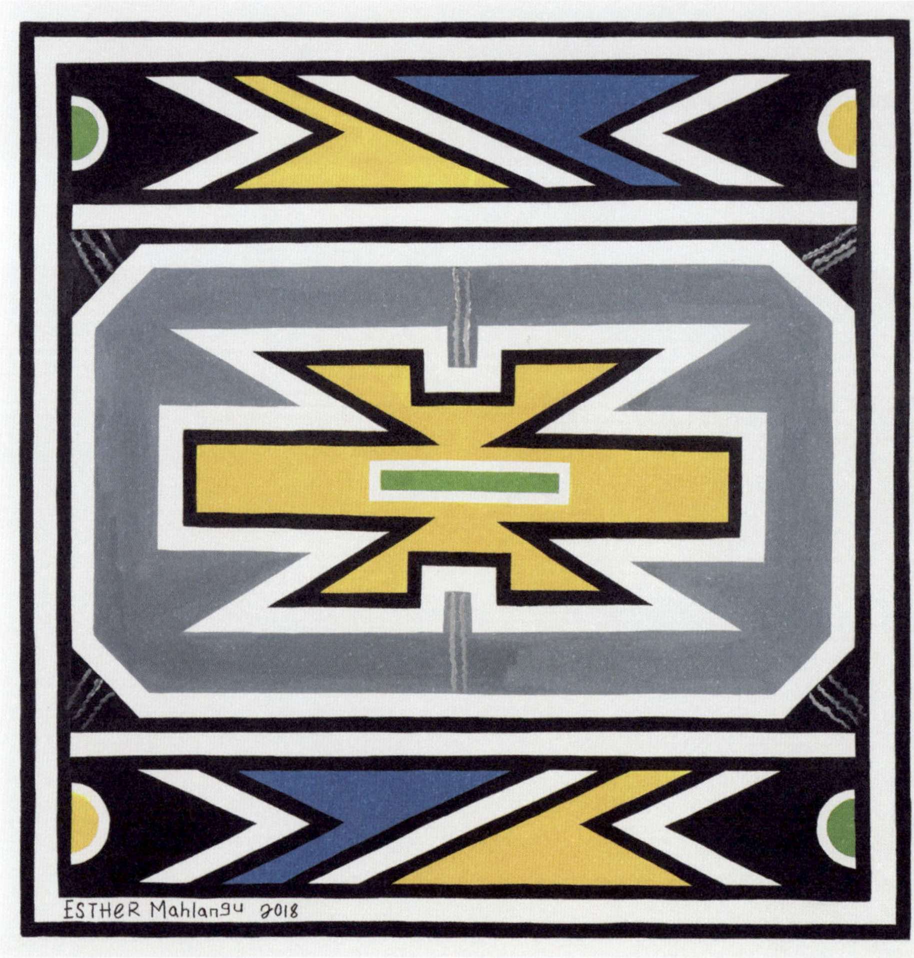
ESTHER Mahlangu 2018

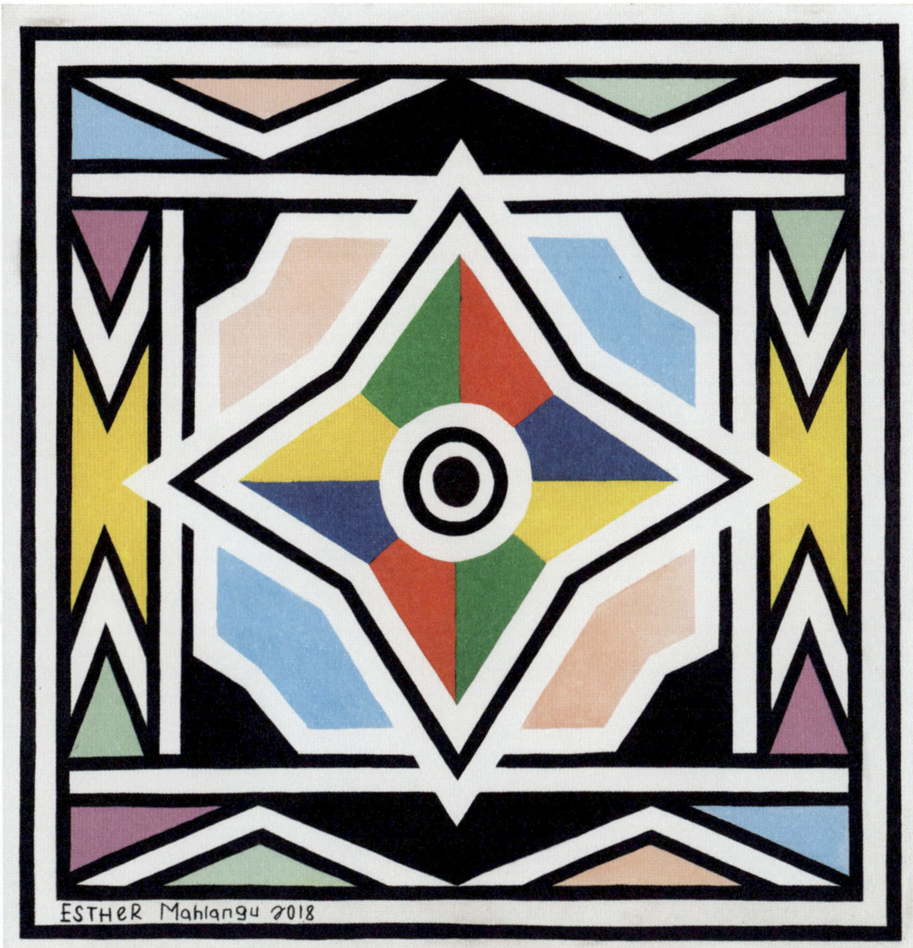
ESTHeR Mahlangu 2018

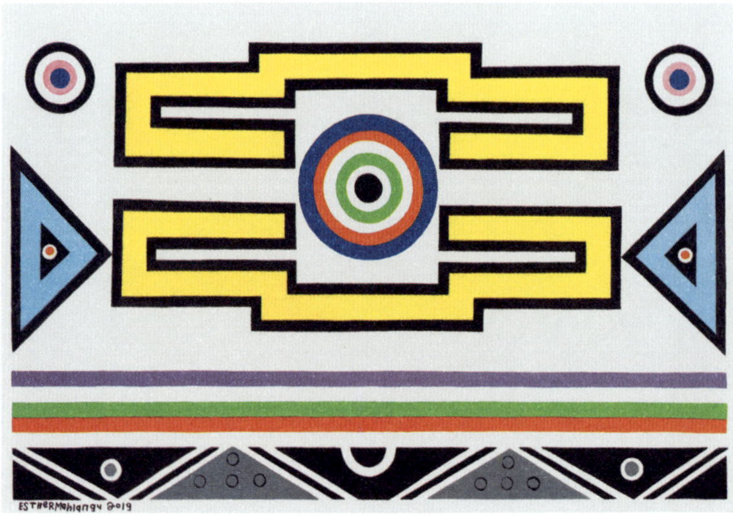
ESTHERMahlangu 2019

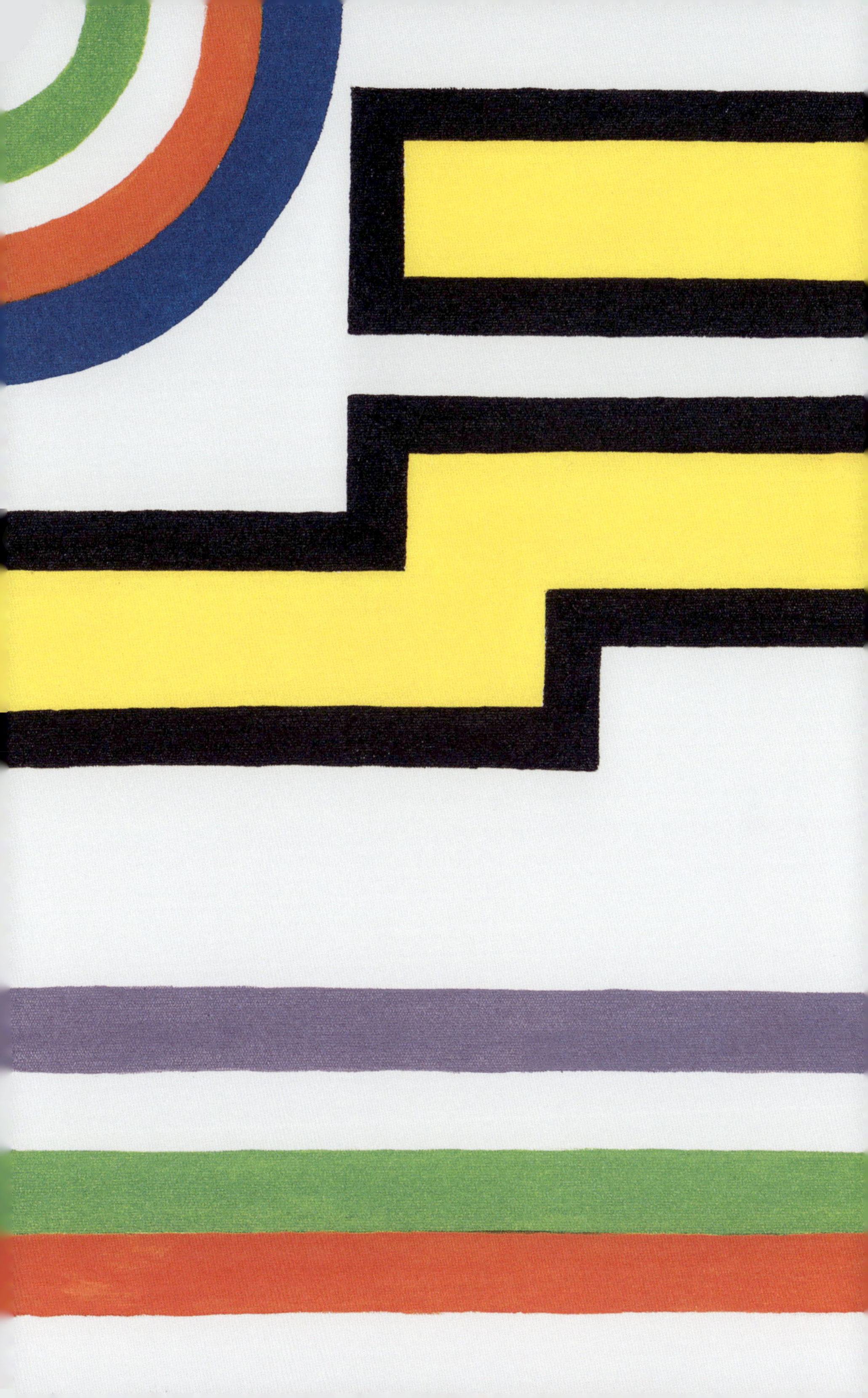

The colours are taken from
the earth ... It lasts for a very long
time. Even storms and heavy rain
cannot wash the art away.

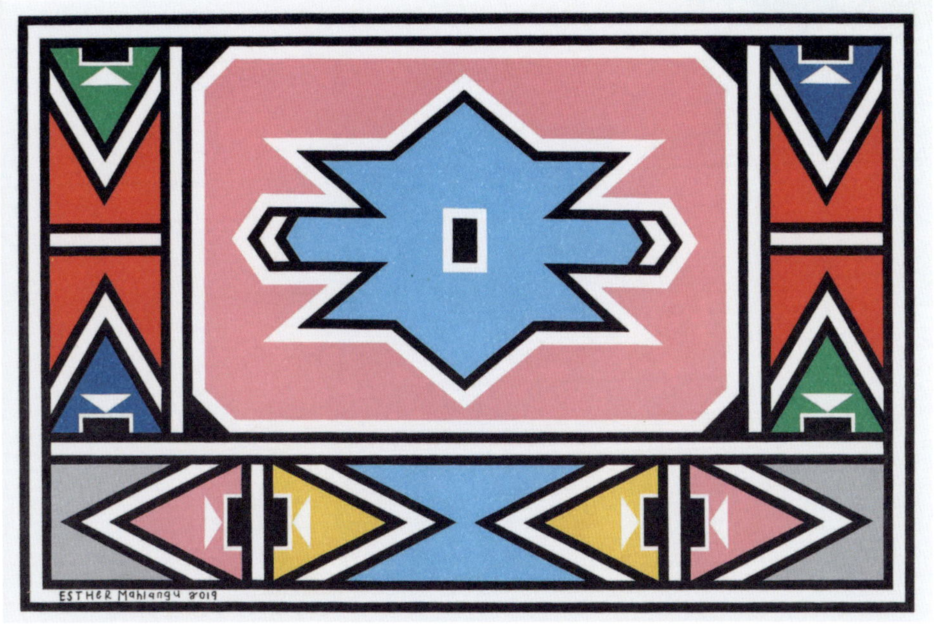
ESTHER Mahlangu 2019

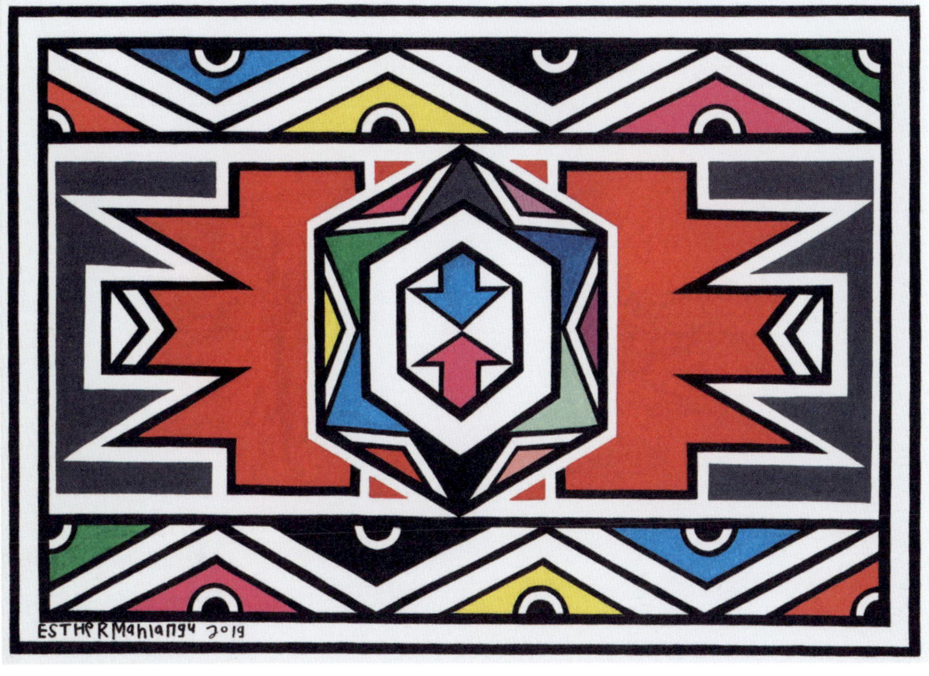
ESTHER Mahlangu 2019

Long after
I am not here anymore,
people will still go and see the
paintings and they will remember
there was an artist called
Esther Mahlangu.

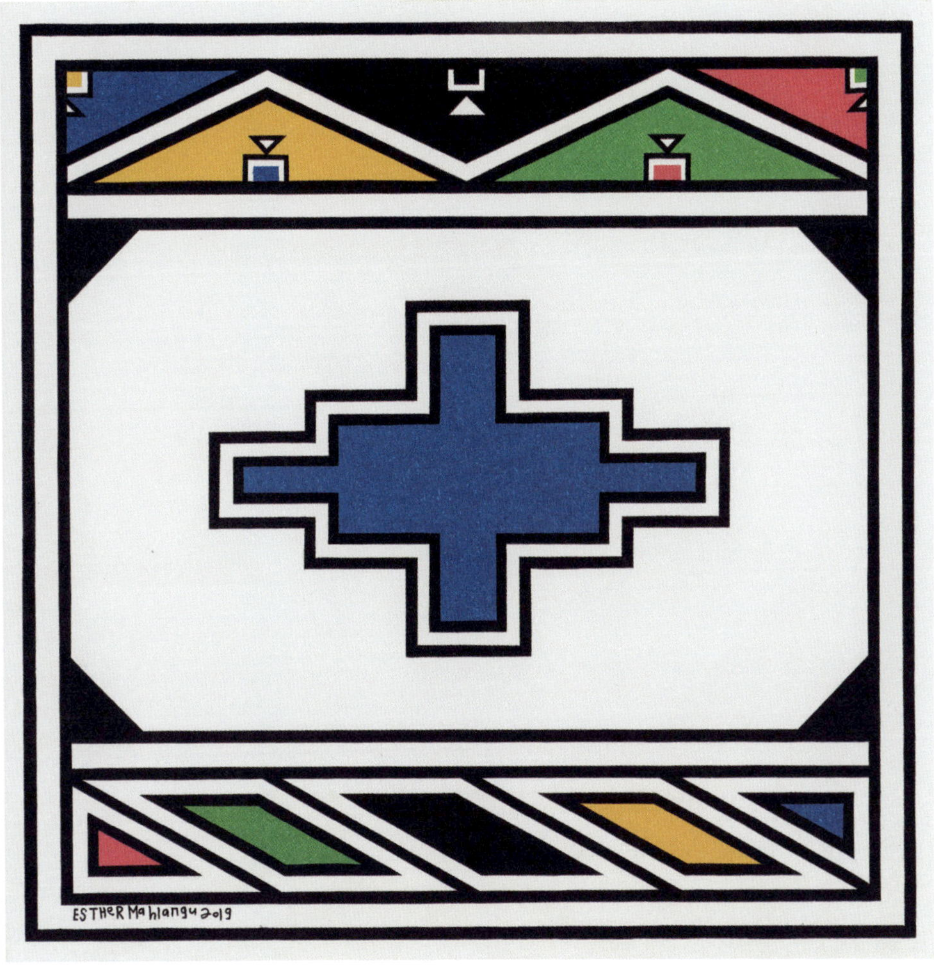
ESTHER Mahlangu 2019

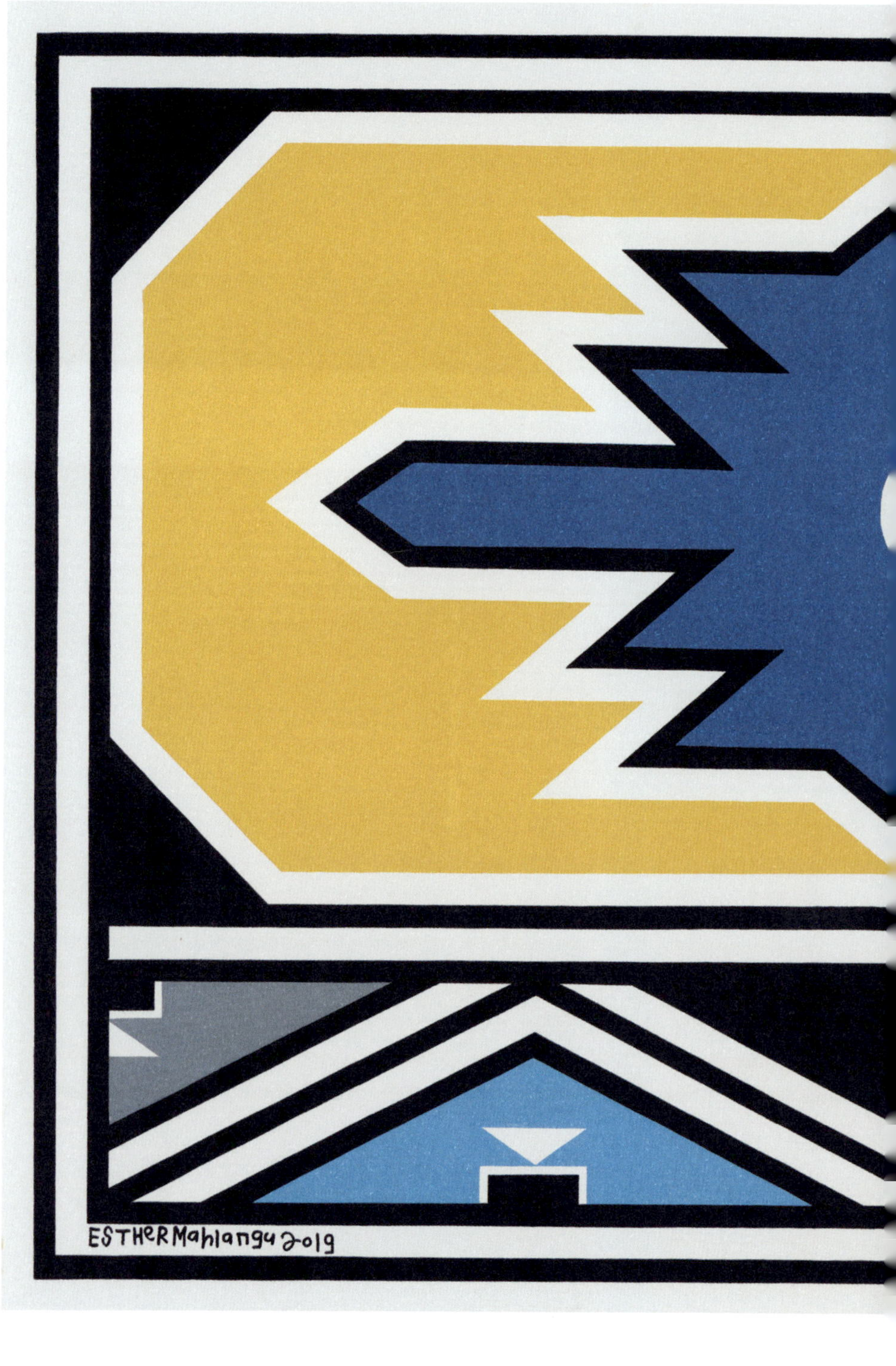
ESTHER Mahlangu 2019

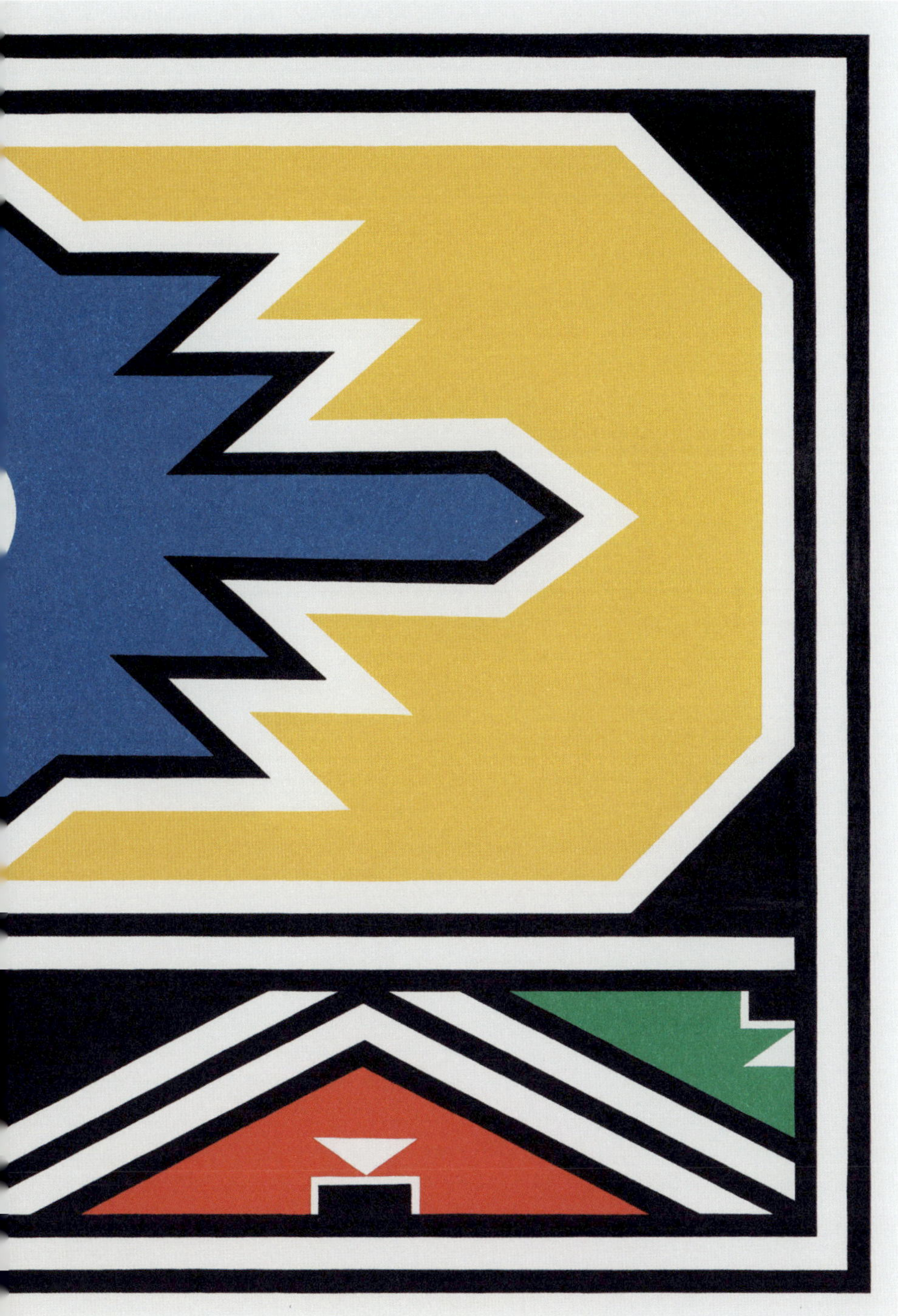

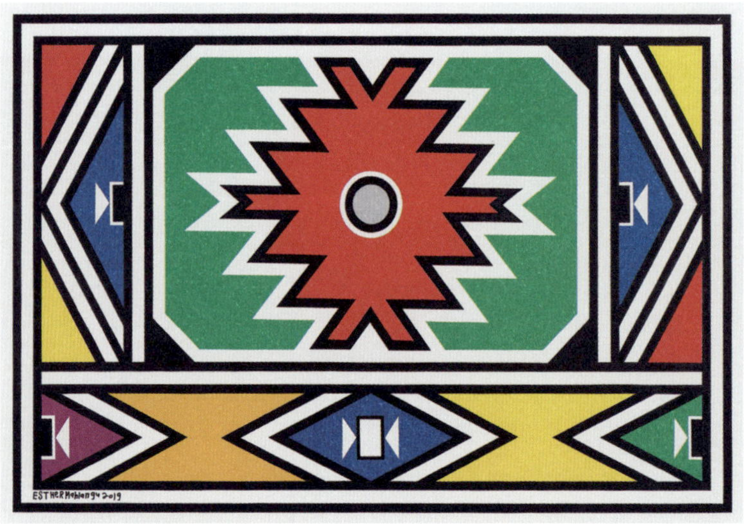
ESTHER Mahlangu 2019

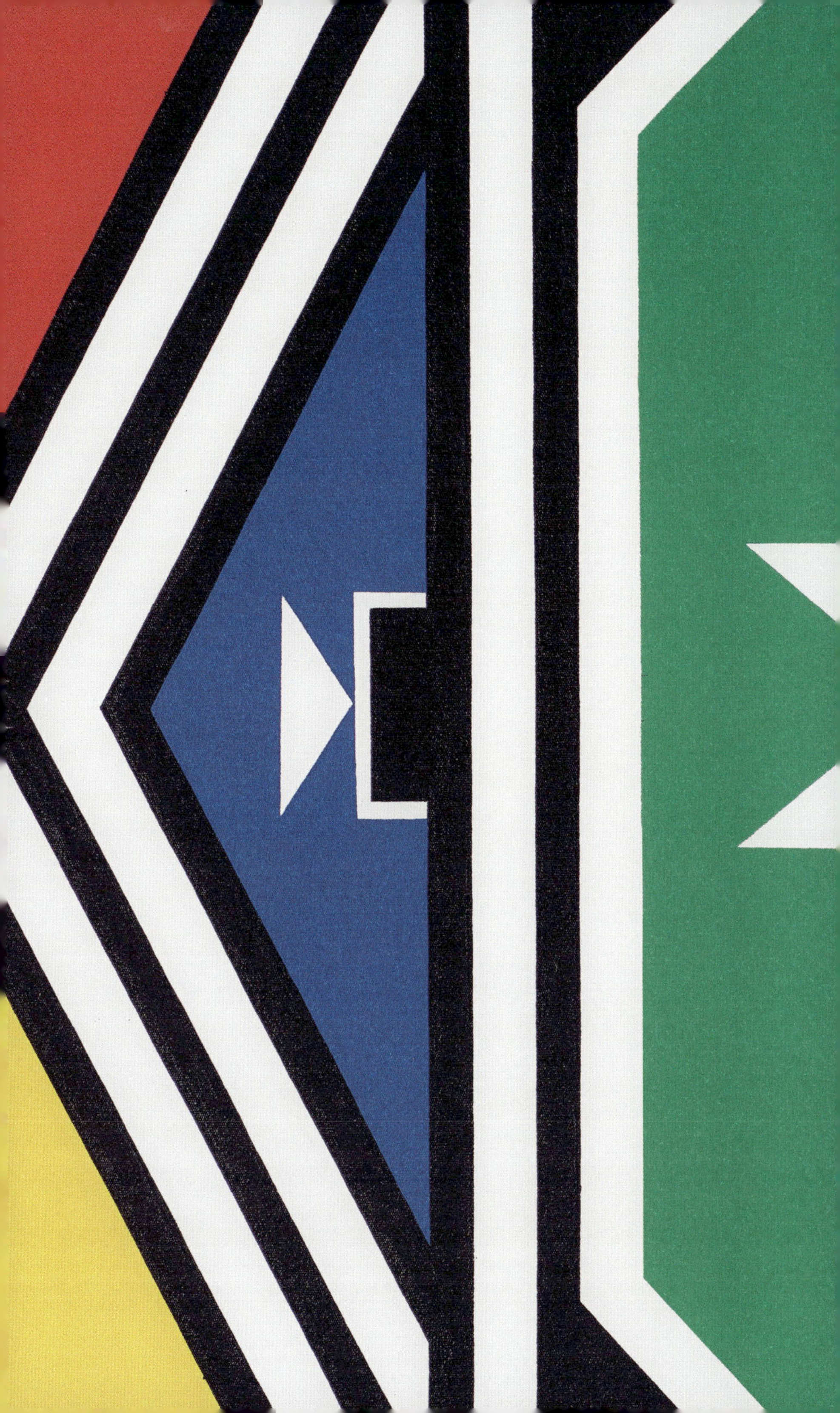

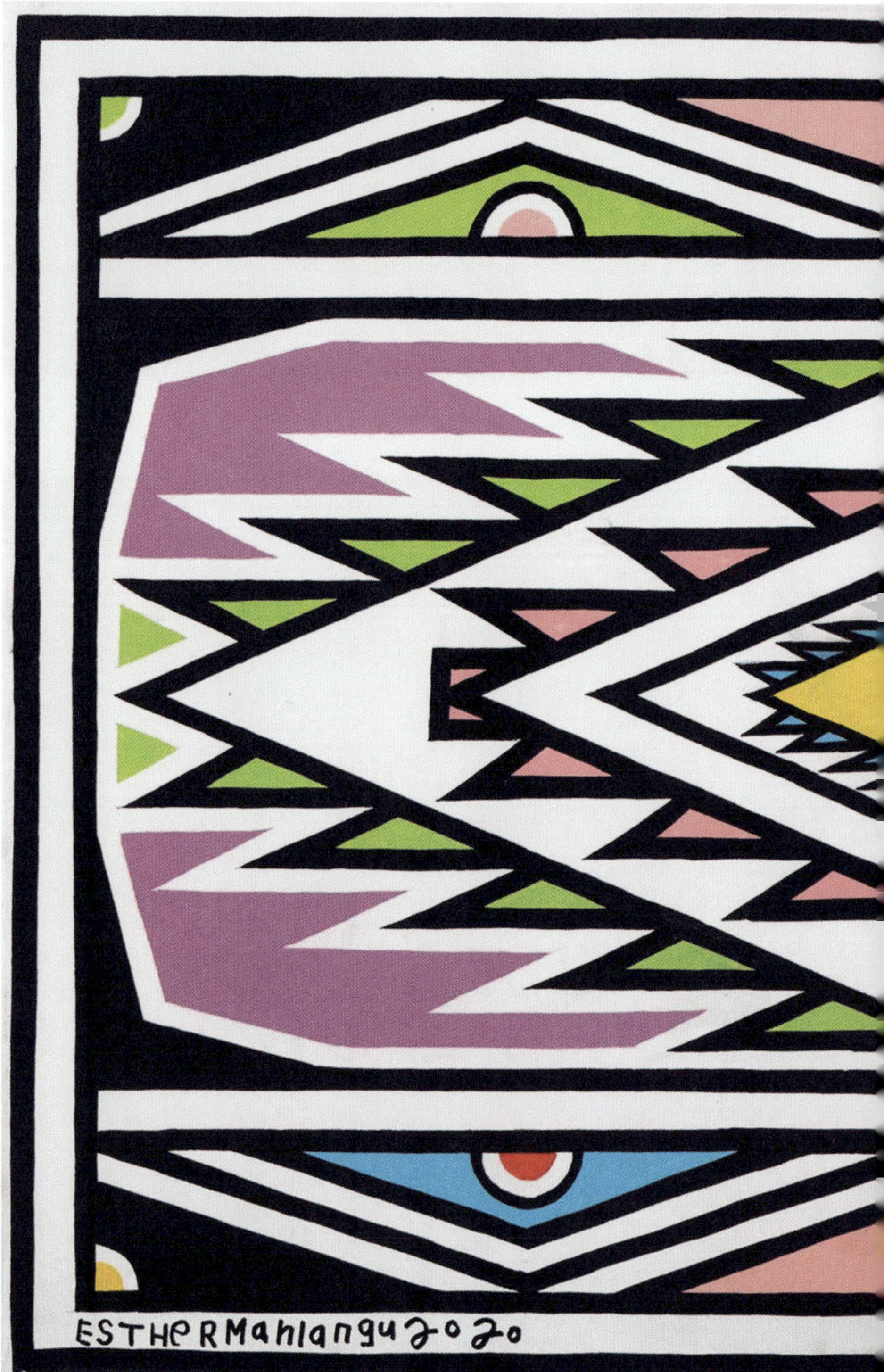
ESTHER Mahlangu 2020

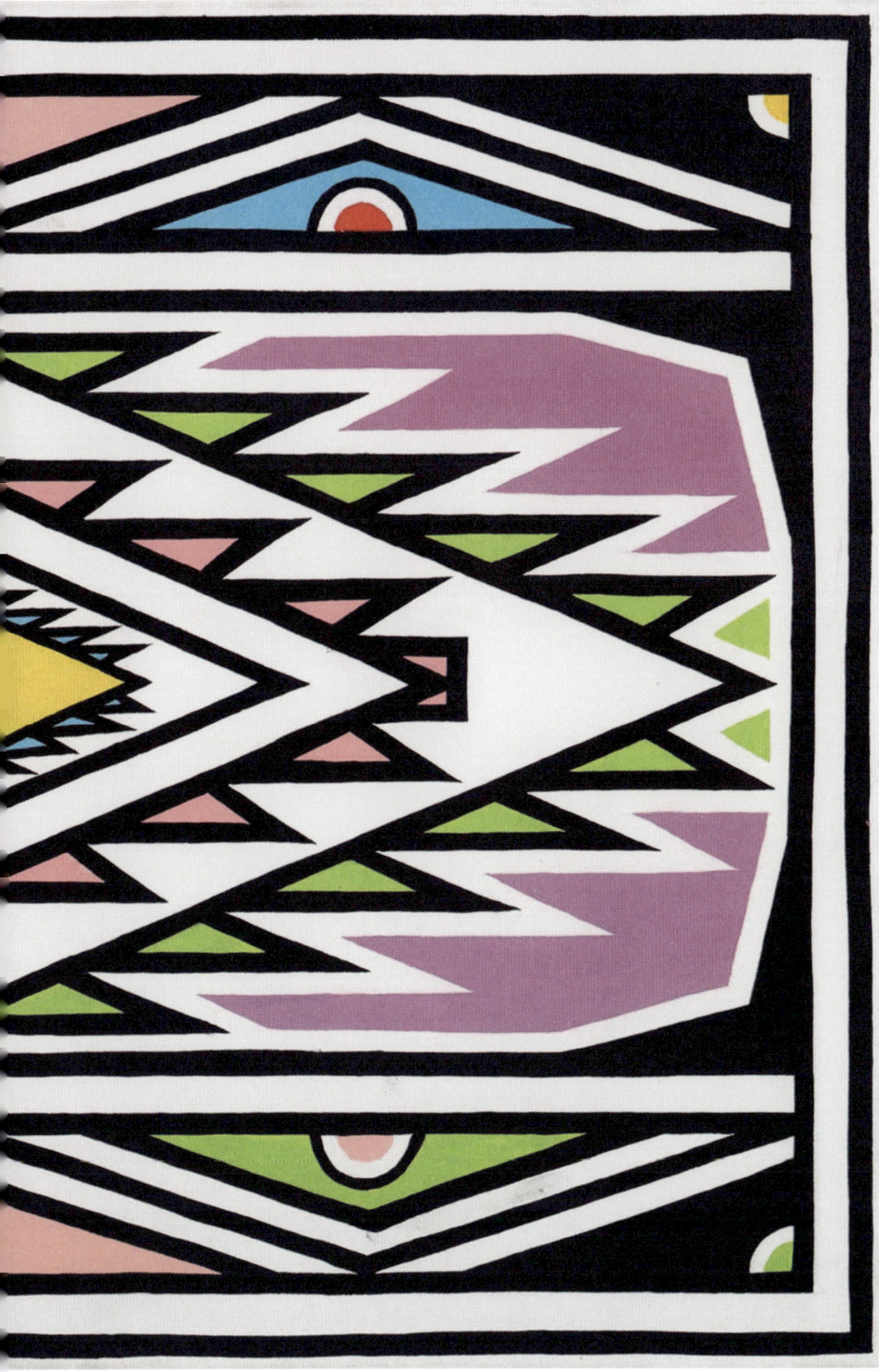

When I am painting,
my heart is very wide.
It reaches out to everything
and everyone.

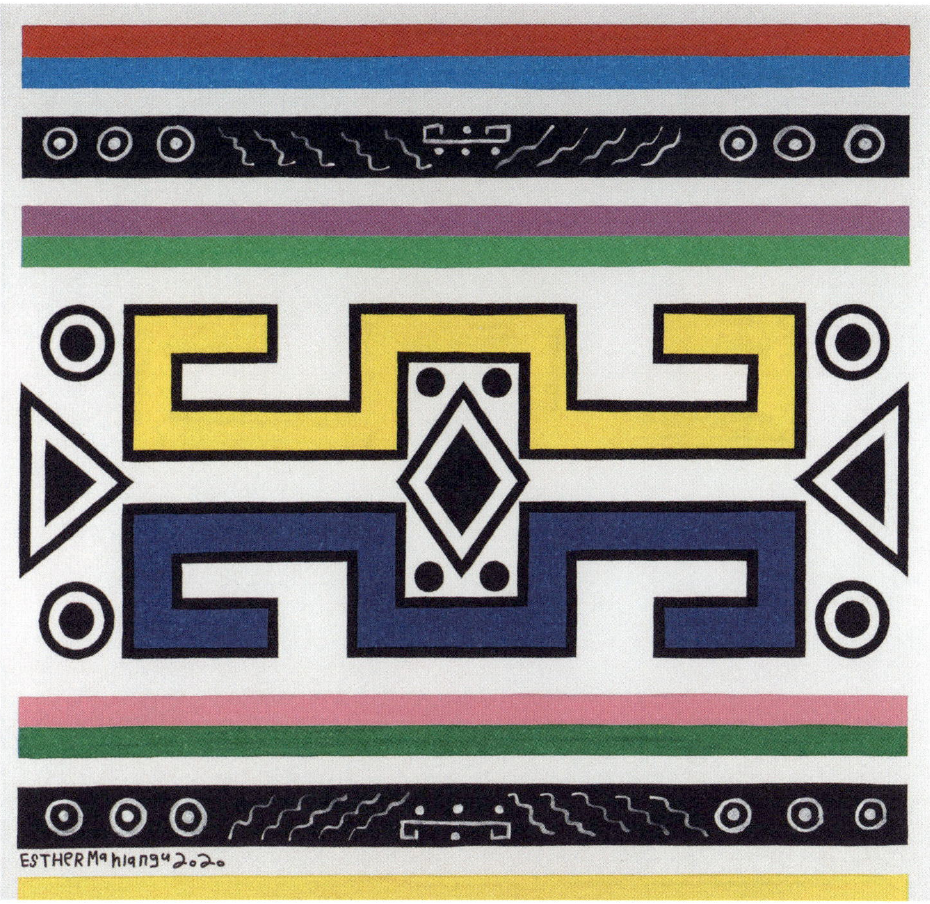
ESTHER Mahlangu 2020

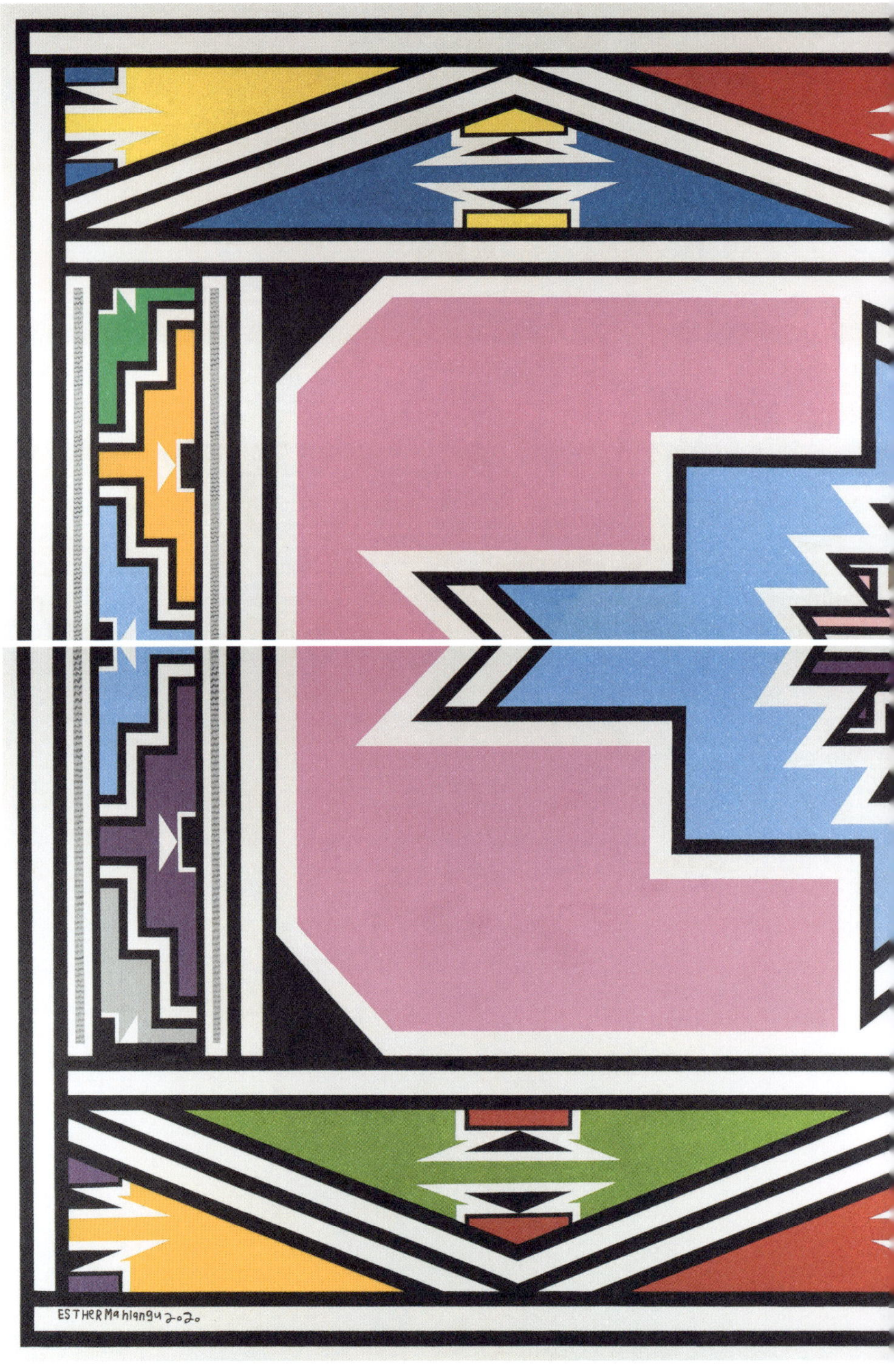
ESTHER Mahlangu 2020

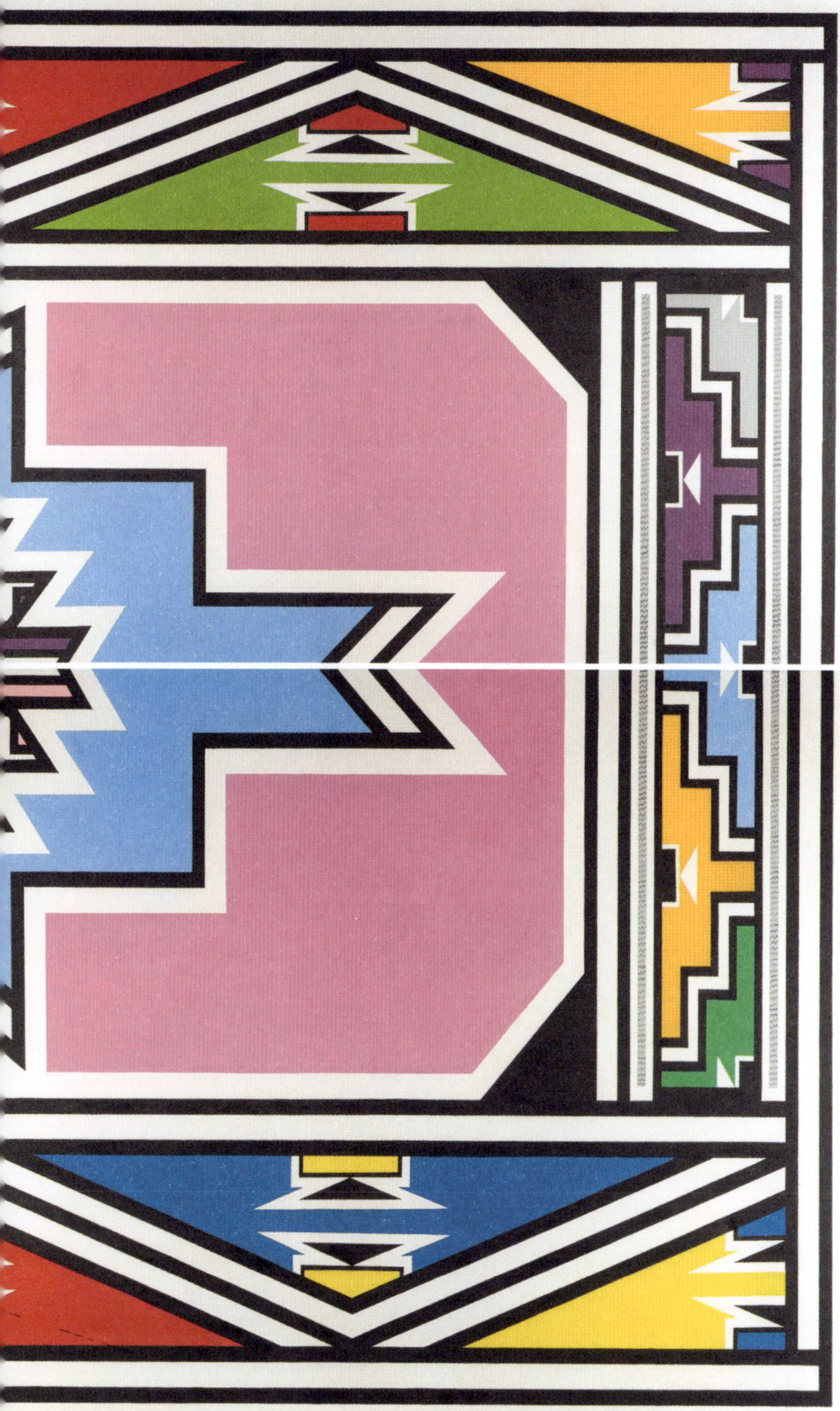

I want to be remembered
for my work, for my paintings.
And for the many places my
art has taken me.

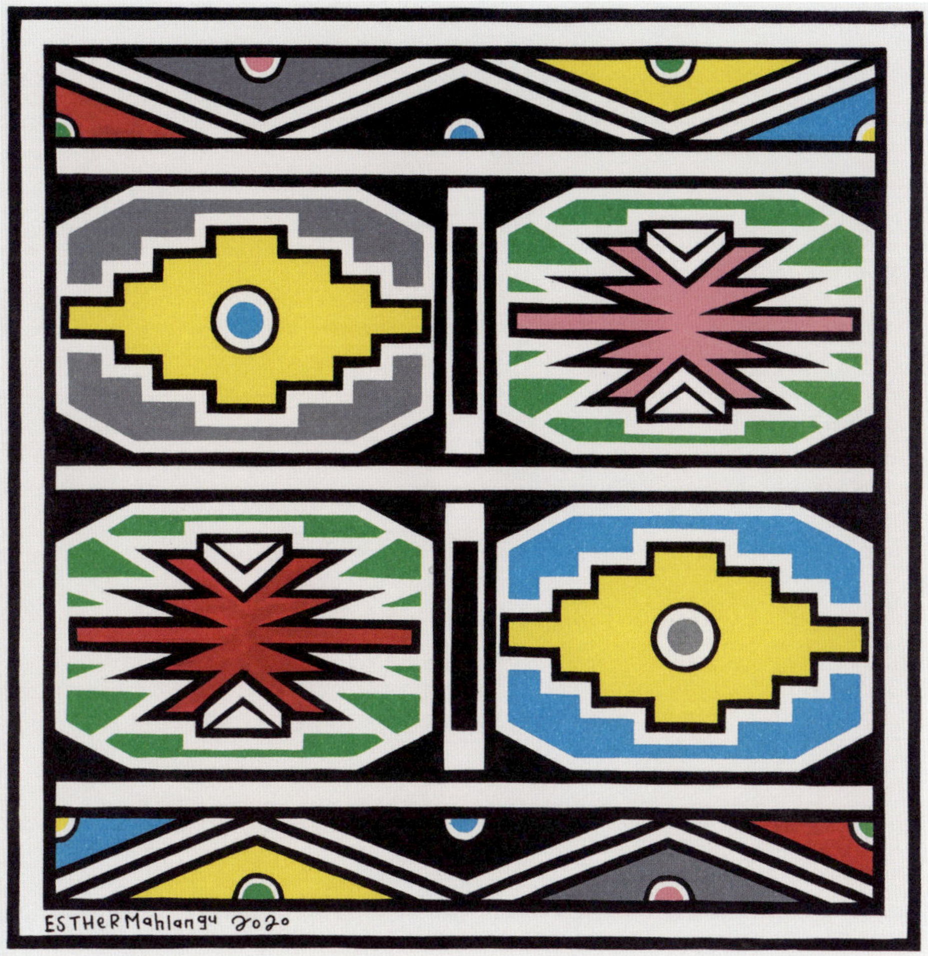
ESTHER Mahlangu 2020

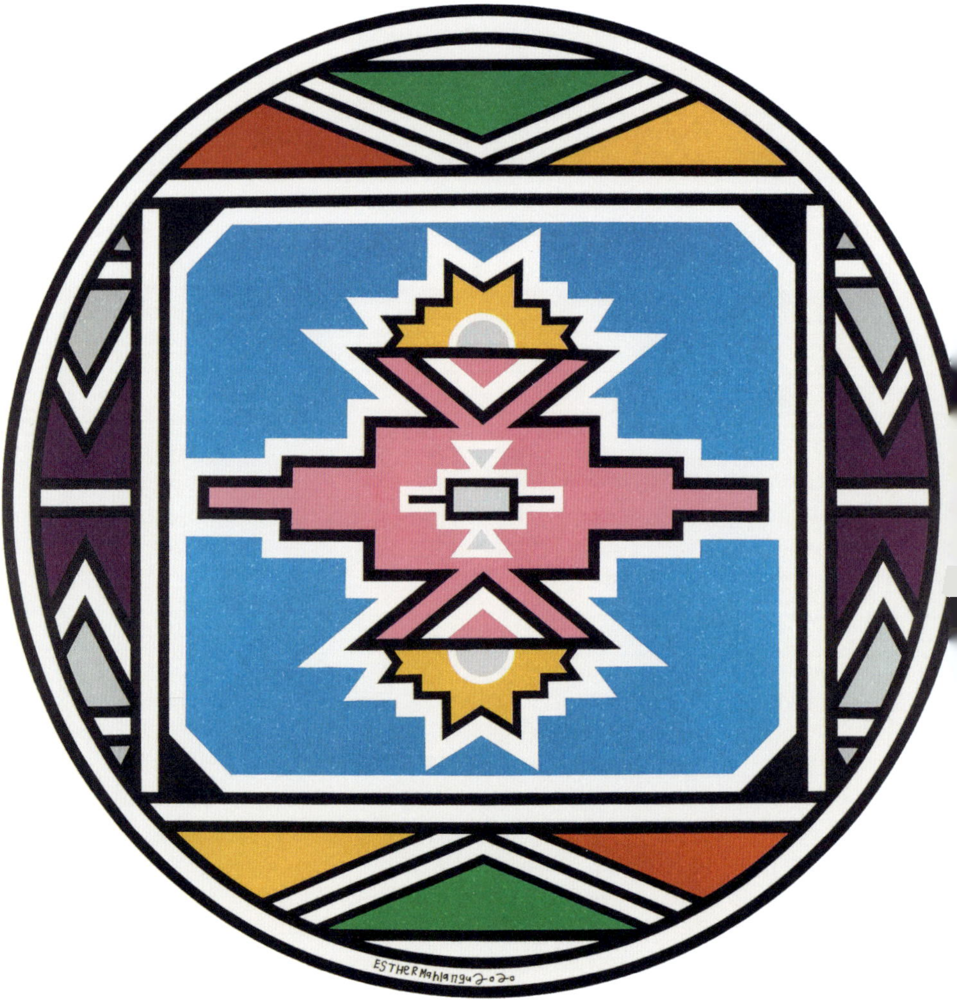
ESTHER Mahlangu 2020

As a self-taught artist,
out of necessity, art becomes
your lifestyle. For me, this
is much better than just an
academic qualification
in the arts.

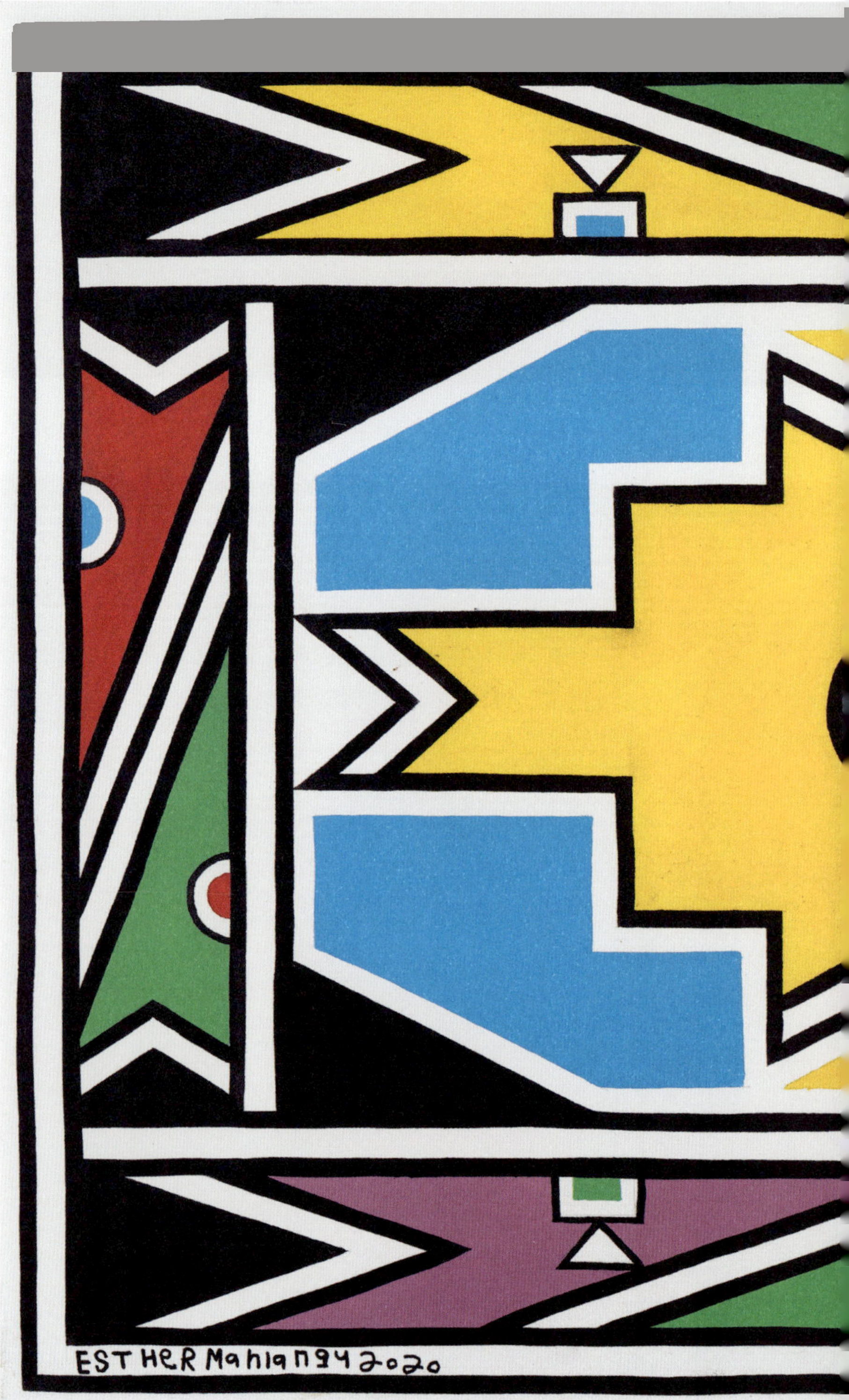
ESTHER Mahlangu 2020

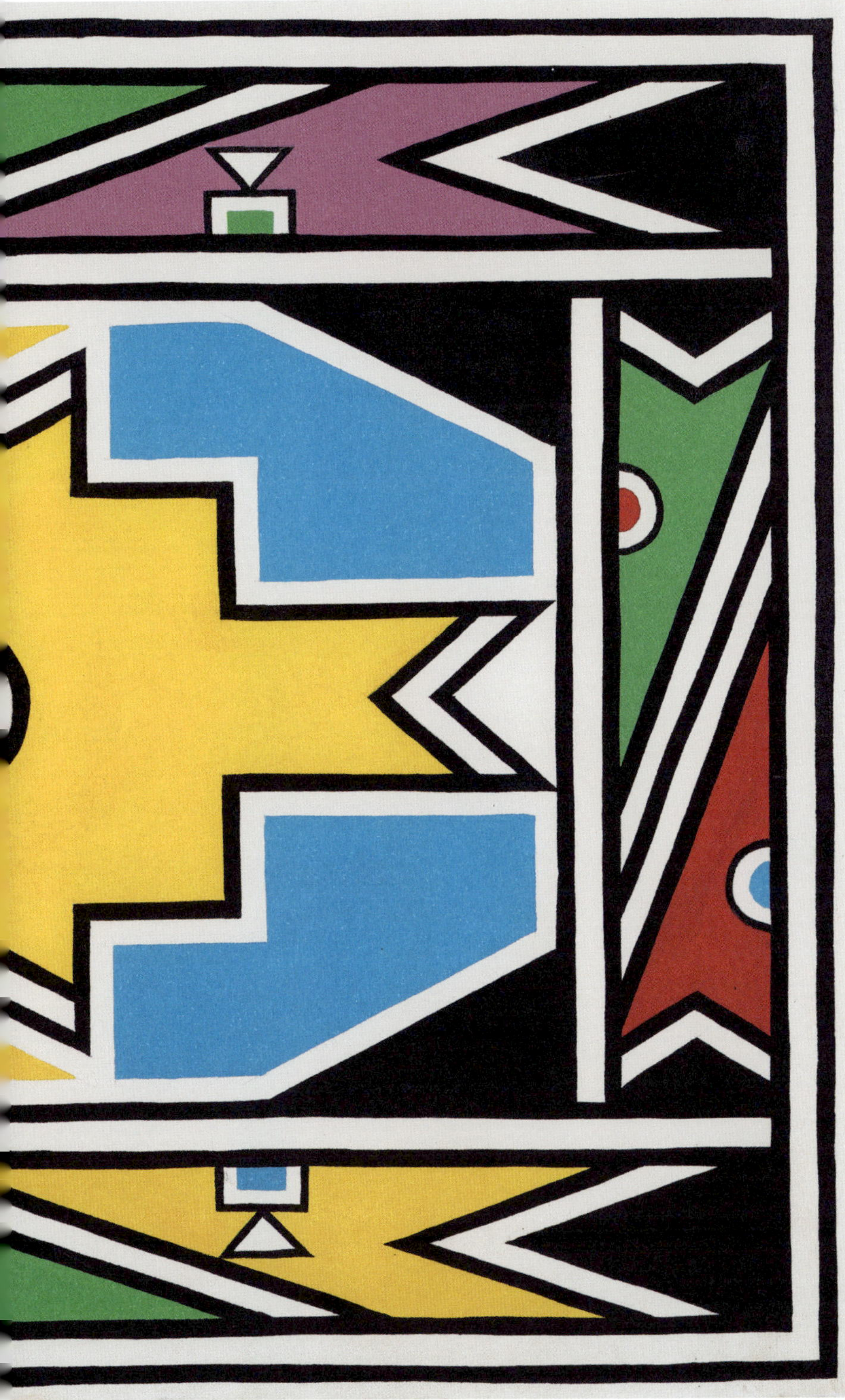

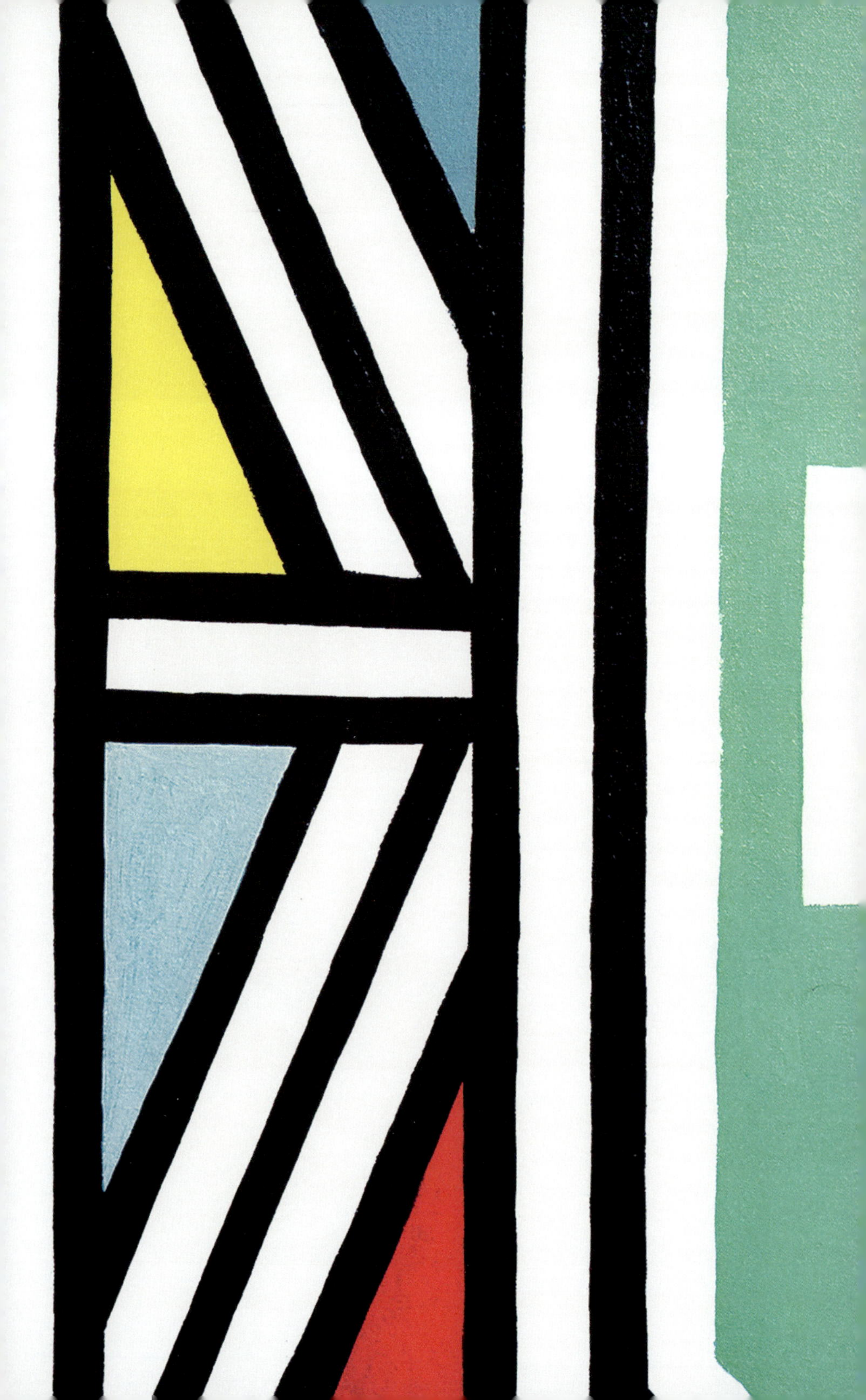

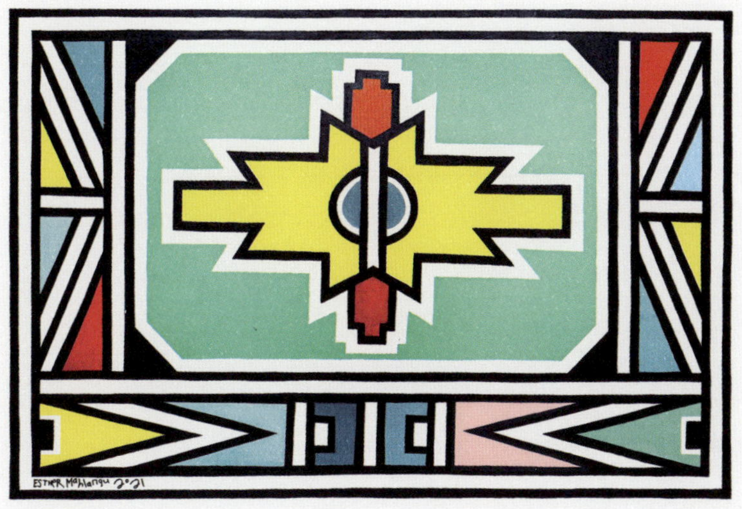
ESTHER Mahlangu 2021

The most important thing is
that the artwork must catch your eye.
I always want to make something
that looks beautiful.

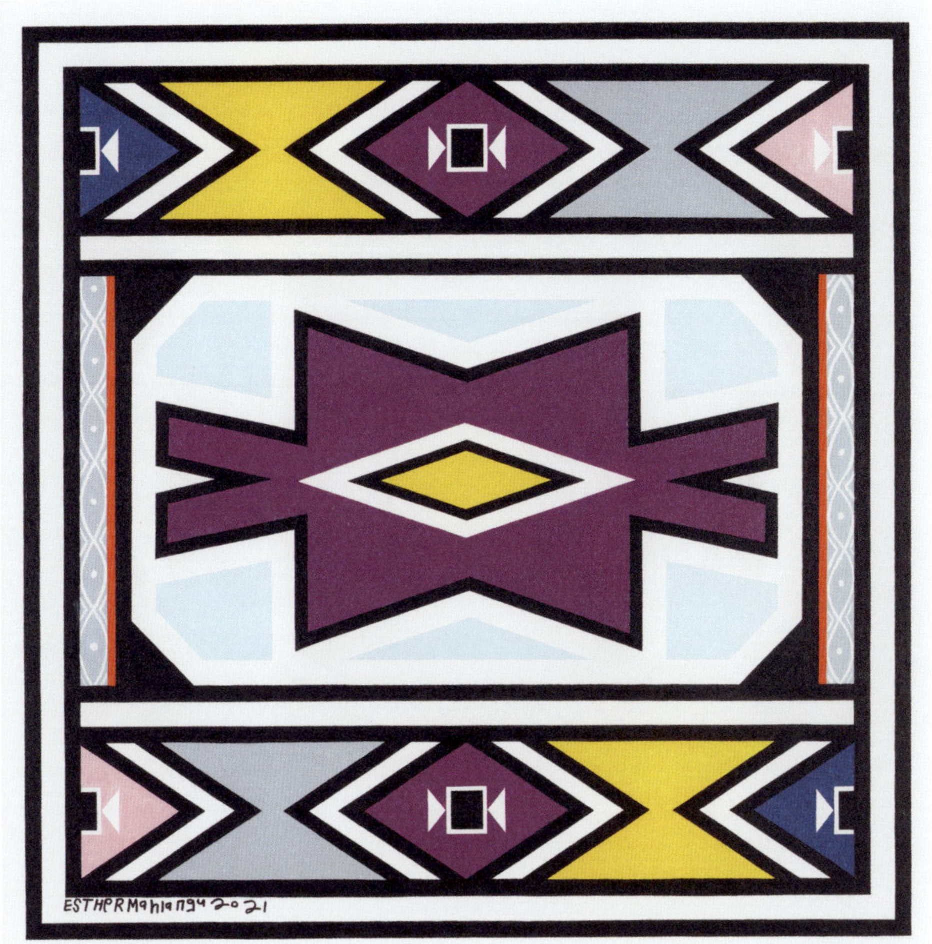
ESTHER Mahlangu 2021

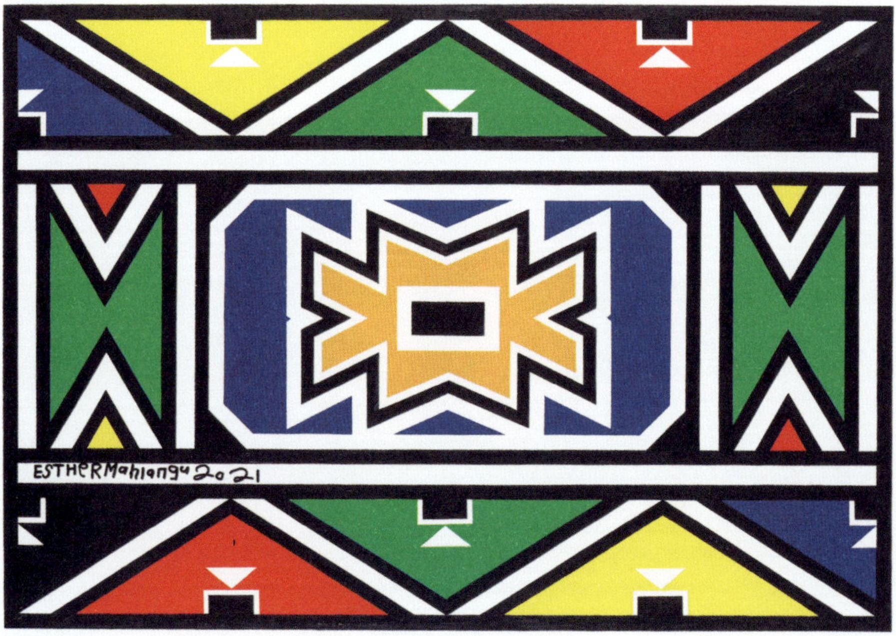
ESTHER Mahlangu 2021

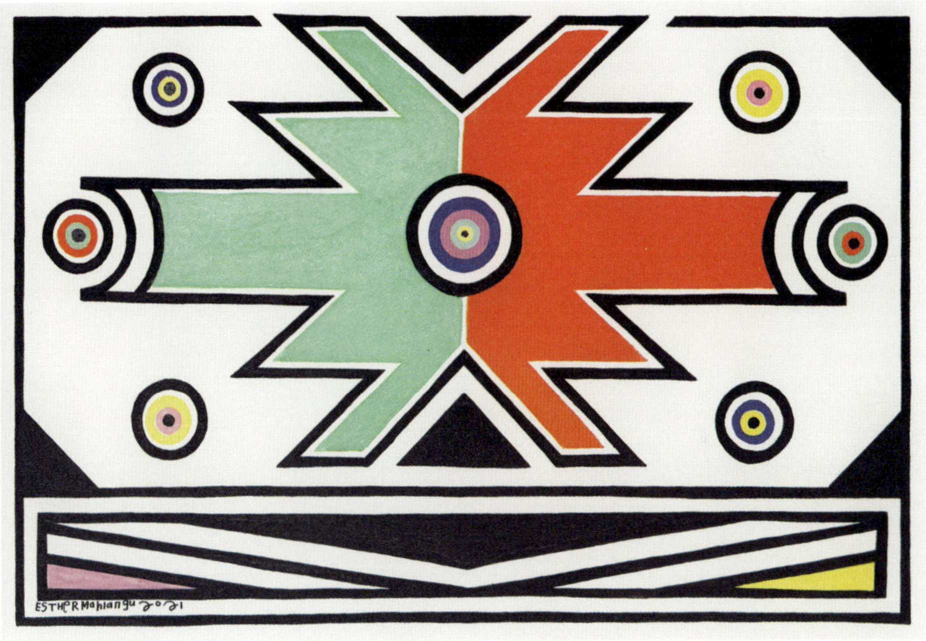
ESTHER Mahlangu 2021

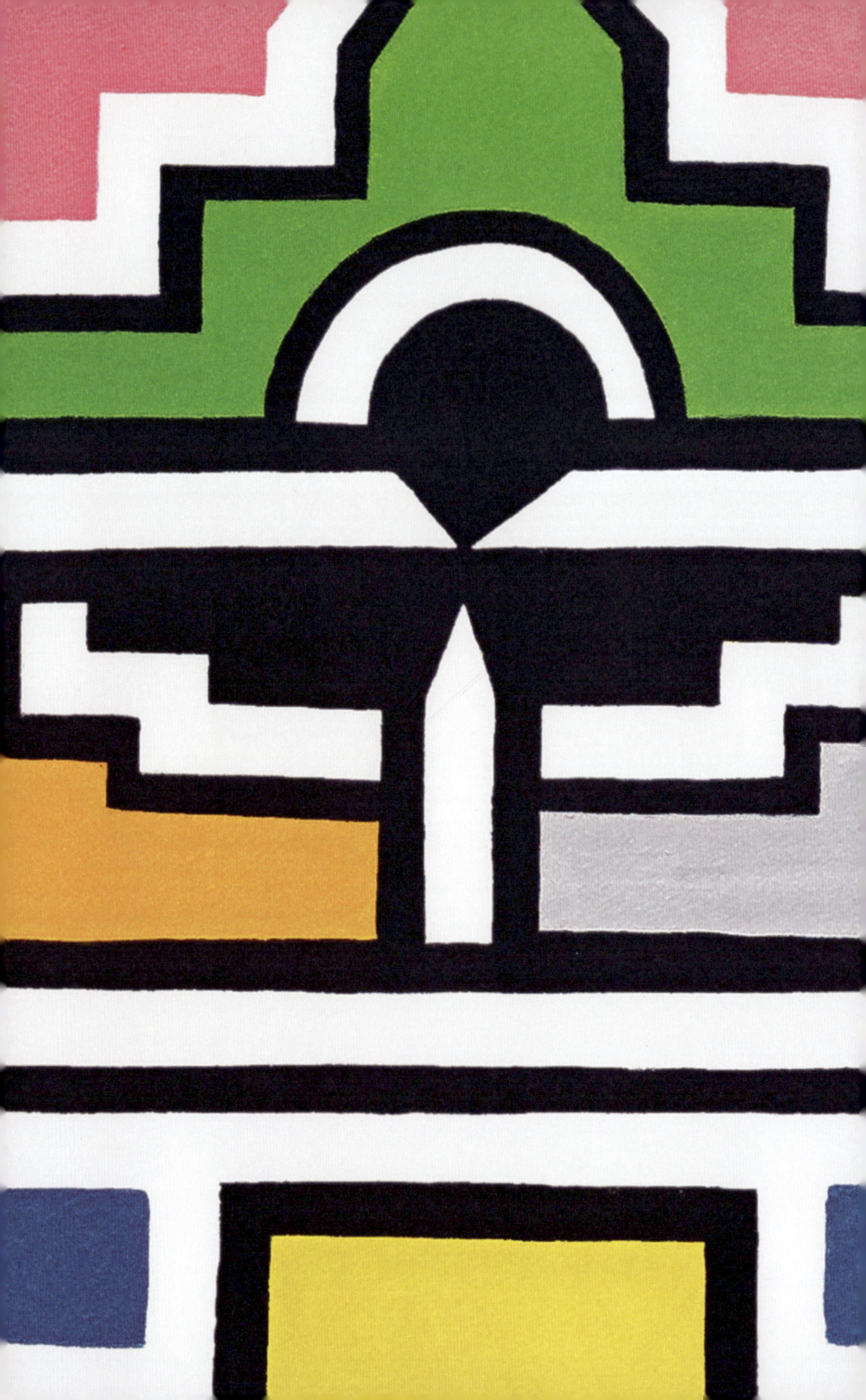

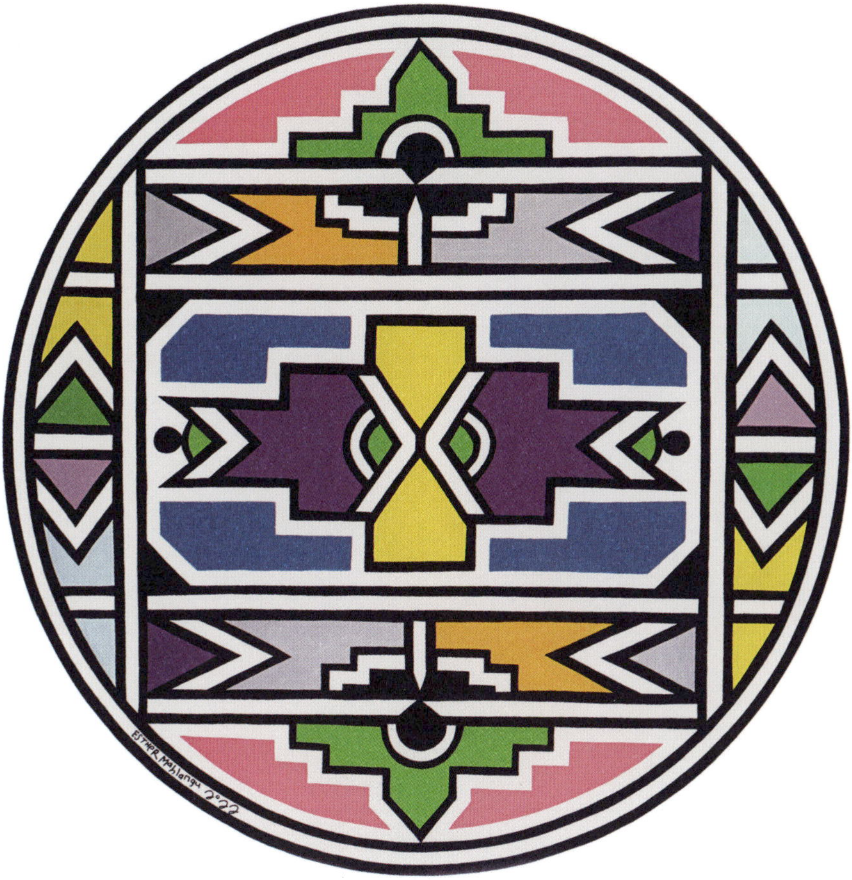
ESTHER Mahlangu 2022

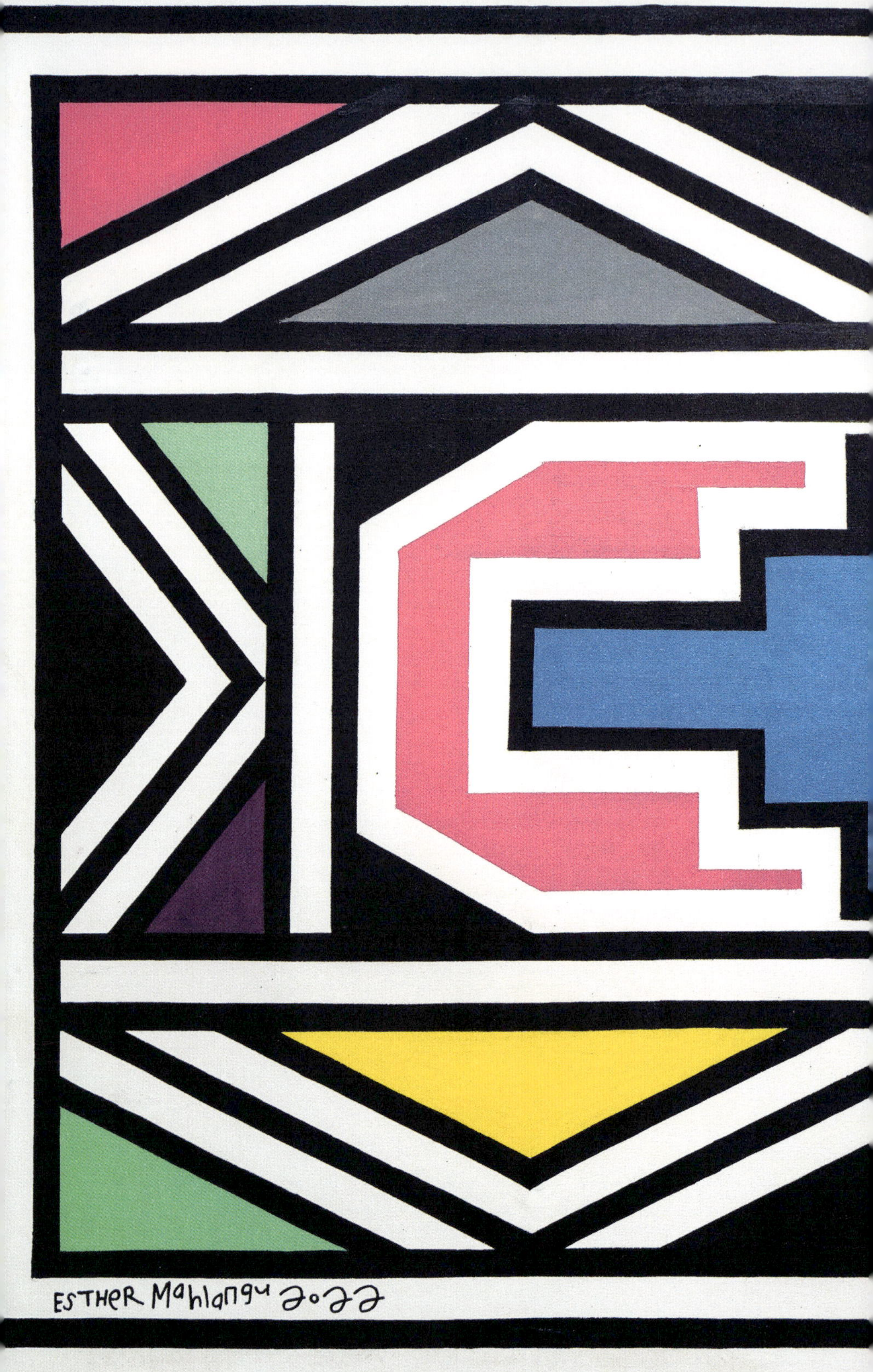
ESTHER Mahlangu 2022

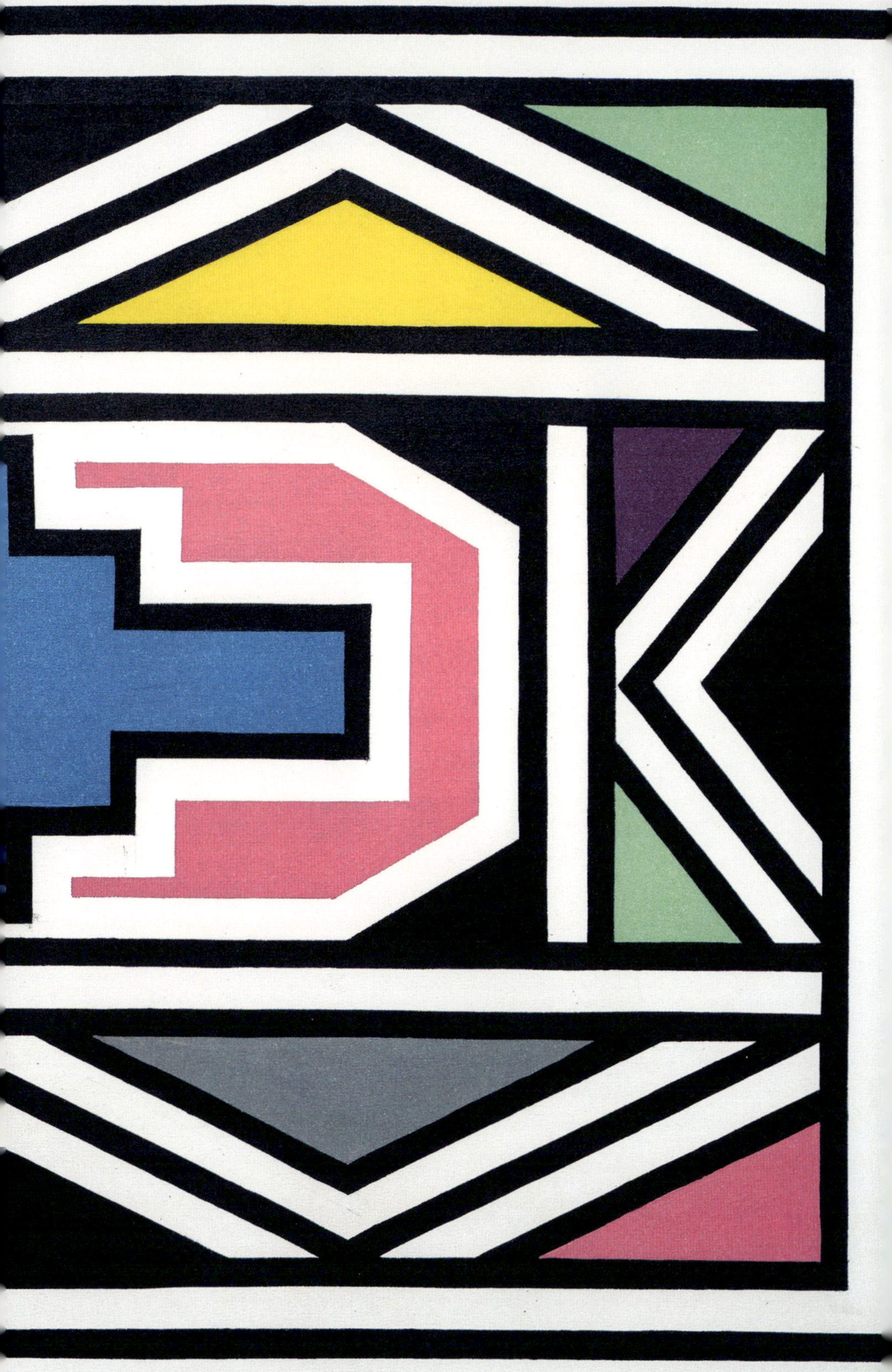

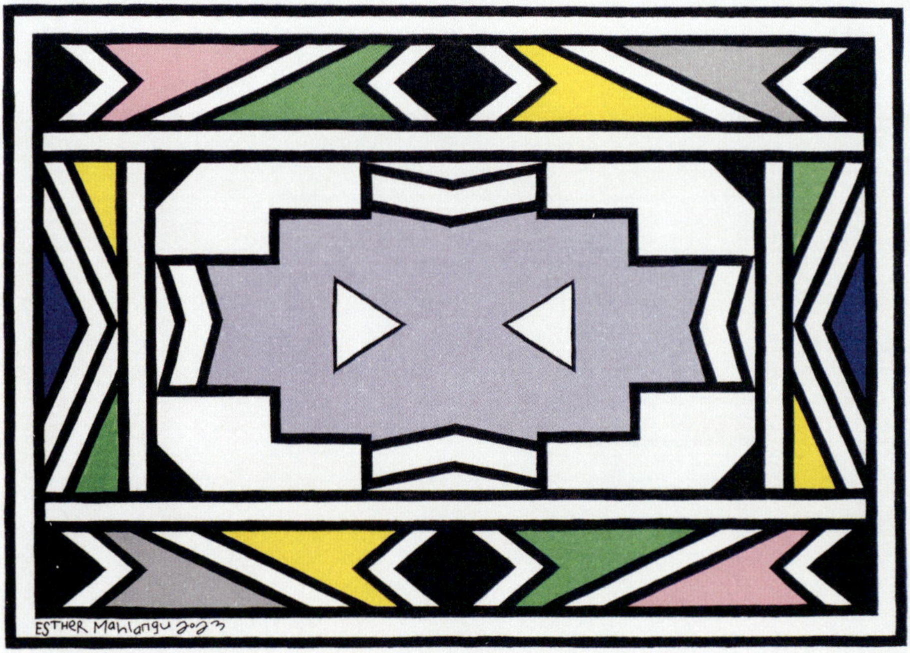
ESTHER Mahlangu 2023

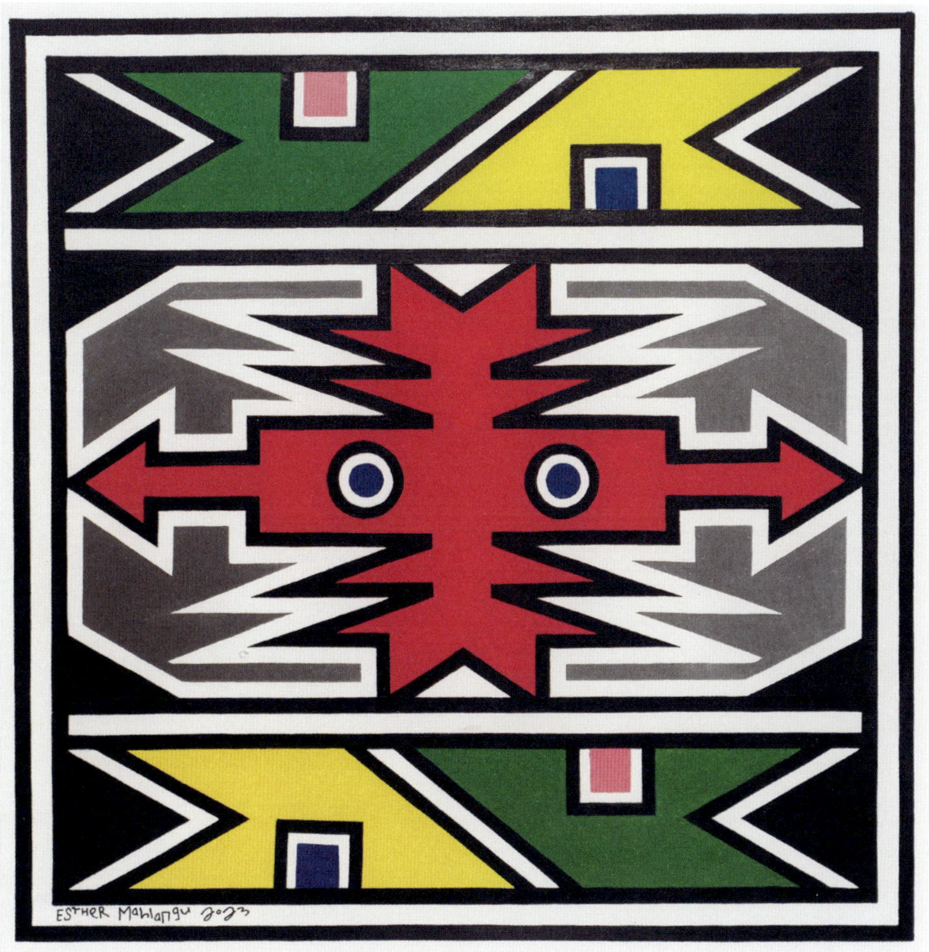
ESTHER Mahlangu 2023

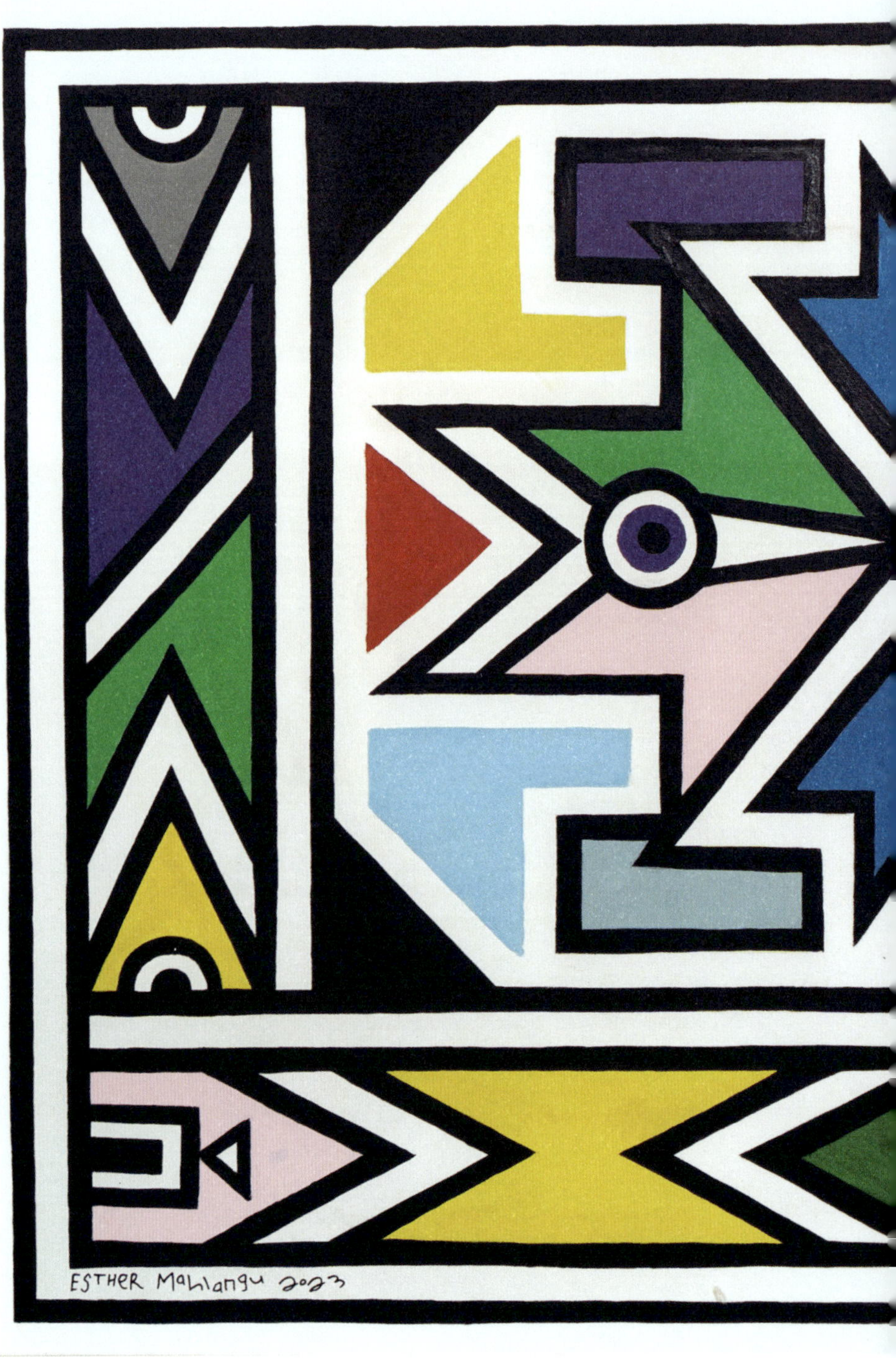
ESTHER Mahlangu 2023

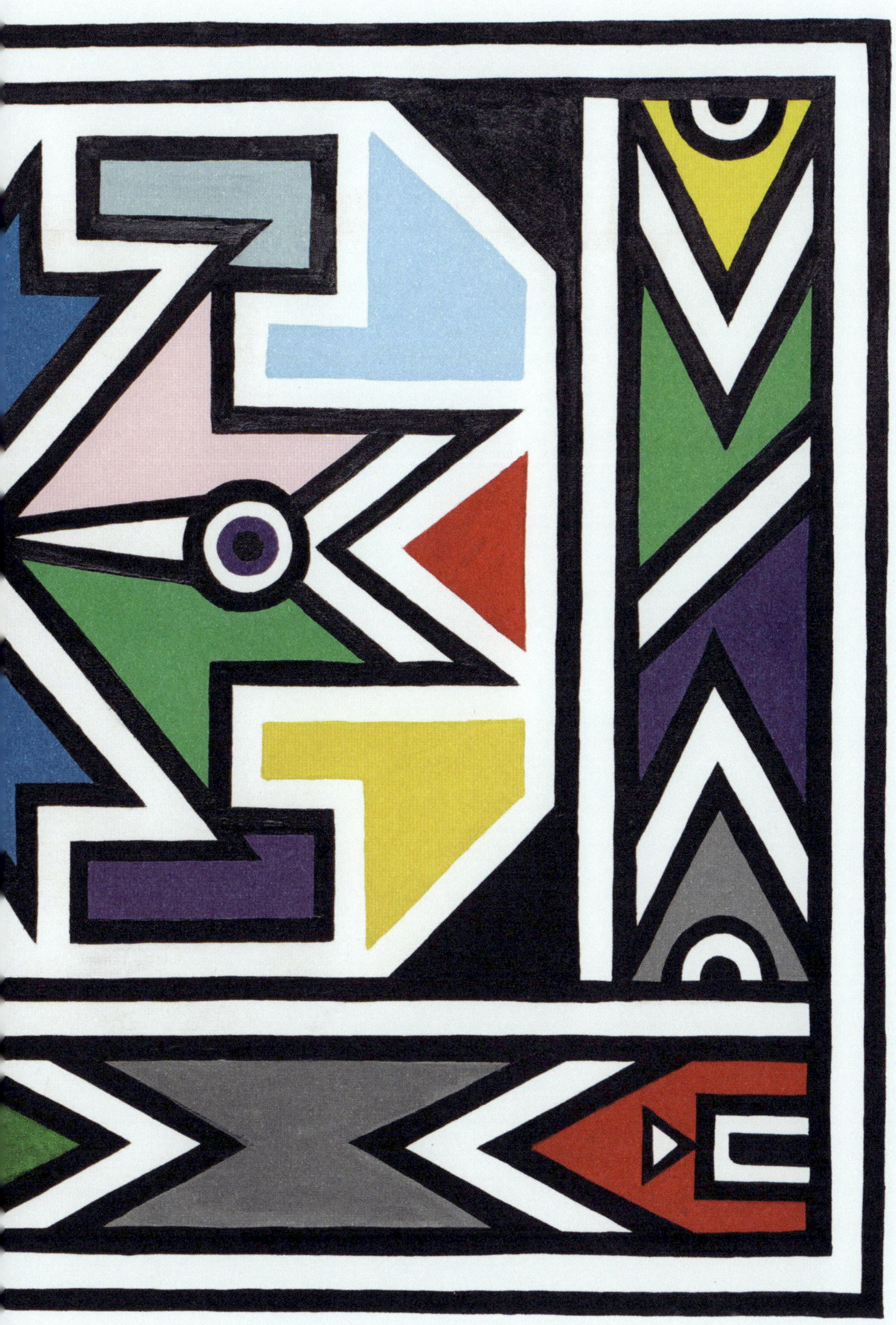

KGARI ESTHER MAHLANGU

Pitika Ntuli

Her brush dances with colours
Capturing her Ndebele history
Where culture and tradition thrive
She paints with passion
To keep her heritage alive
Hand steady as a measuring rod
Throughout apartheid times
Her murals a flag of hope
Bold strokes and intricate patterns
Geometric images smiling in bright colours

Fingerprints of her canvases
Each brushstroke tells a story
Pulsating with emotions
Inspired by her Ndebele heritage
She weaves a visual tale
Preserving the richness
In her art that will endure

Geometric precision guides
Her artistic hand
Creating a symphony of colours
A visual wonderland
From walls to canvases
Her art knows no bounds
Spreading cultural richness
Her talent sings in bright colours
In deep conversation with us

A beacon with artistic grace
Her work transcends borders
Connecting place and spirit
Sharing her soul
Leaving an indelible mark
A legacy that will forever unfold

We celebrate this remarkable painter
A woman of power and grace
A true artist
Acclaimed for her vibrant strokes,
Enriching the world with her artistic vision
We salute you MumEsther

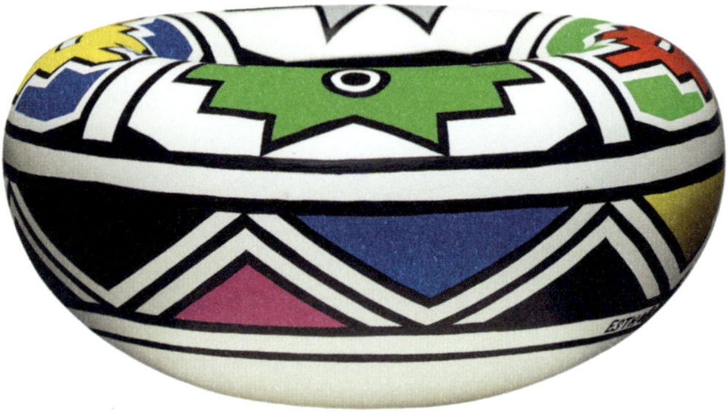

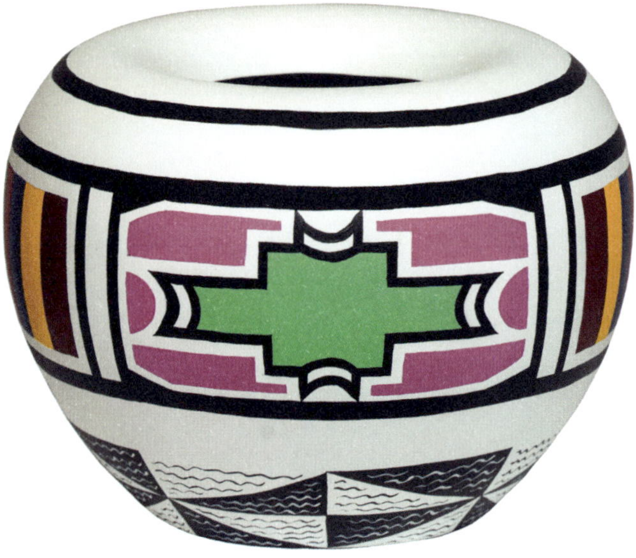

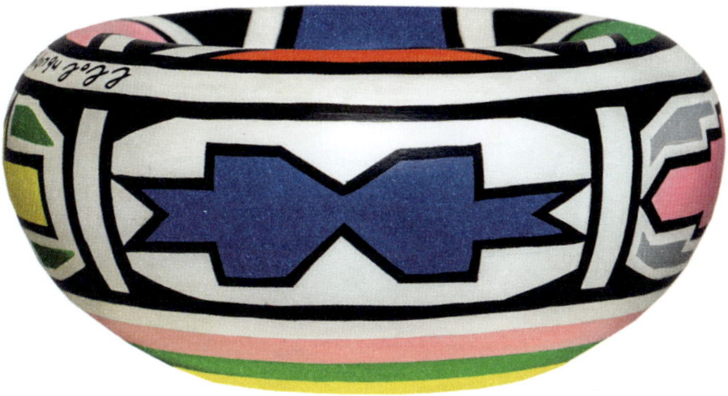

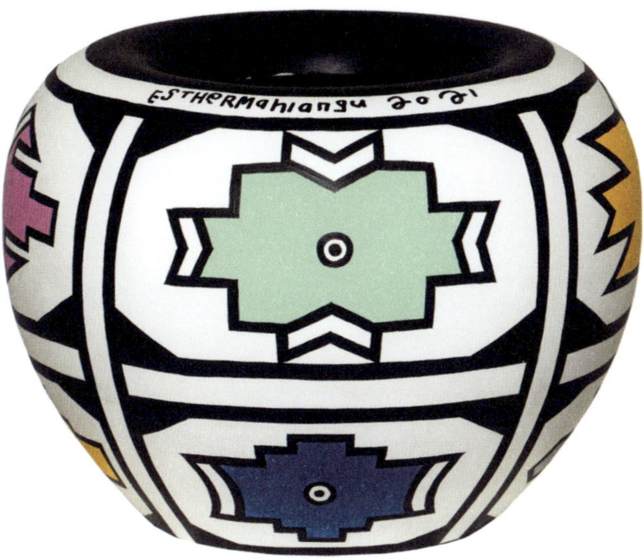
ESTHERMahlangu 2021

FASHIONING CULTURE

Thebe Magugu

'AS CHILDREN GROW UP TODAY, THEY'RE LOSING THEIR CULTURE. I DON'T WANT MY CULTURE TO DIE ... THEY MUST KNOW THEIR CULTURE AND WHERE THEY COME FROM.'

Esther Mahlangu

Throughout time, 'fashion' – within the broader spectrum of the visual art and creative disciplines – has often been relegated to the sphere of mere commerce. This blindly negates the complexity and acuity with which the fashion industry can celebrate the past, reflect the present and foreshadow the future through a series of unique and complex methodologies applied by fashion designers. Fashion is also an unspoken language, where colours, details, trims and silhouettes can summon up swathes of history. However, the most important function of fashion is its ability to transcribe and preserve culture.

I have always held a fascination for the Ndebele, who take great pride in their national identity and sense of dress. The proportions of their garments – which extend their physical form and protrude from various parts of the body – suggest a traditional attire completely untouched by the influence of colonization, creating an avant-garde silhouette not found anywhere else in the world. On these garments, a series of signifiers act as information relaying details about the wearer – age, lineage, ranking – which speak to both the physical and implied layering apparent in the overall attire. From the graphic, colour-blocked, mid-weight blanket ('Nguba/Umbhalo') to the large hoops and cuffs created out of beaded strands of twisted grass that encircle the neck, torso and limbs ('Linrholwani'), and the uniquely designed

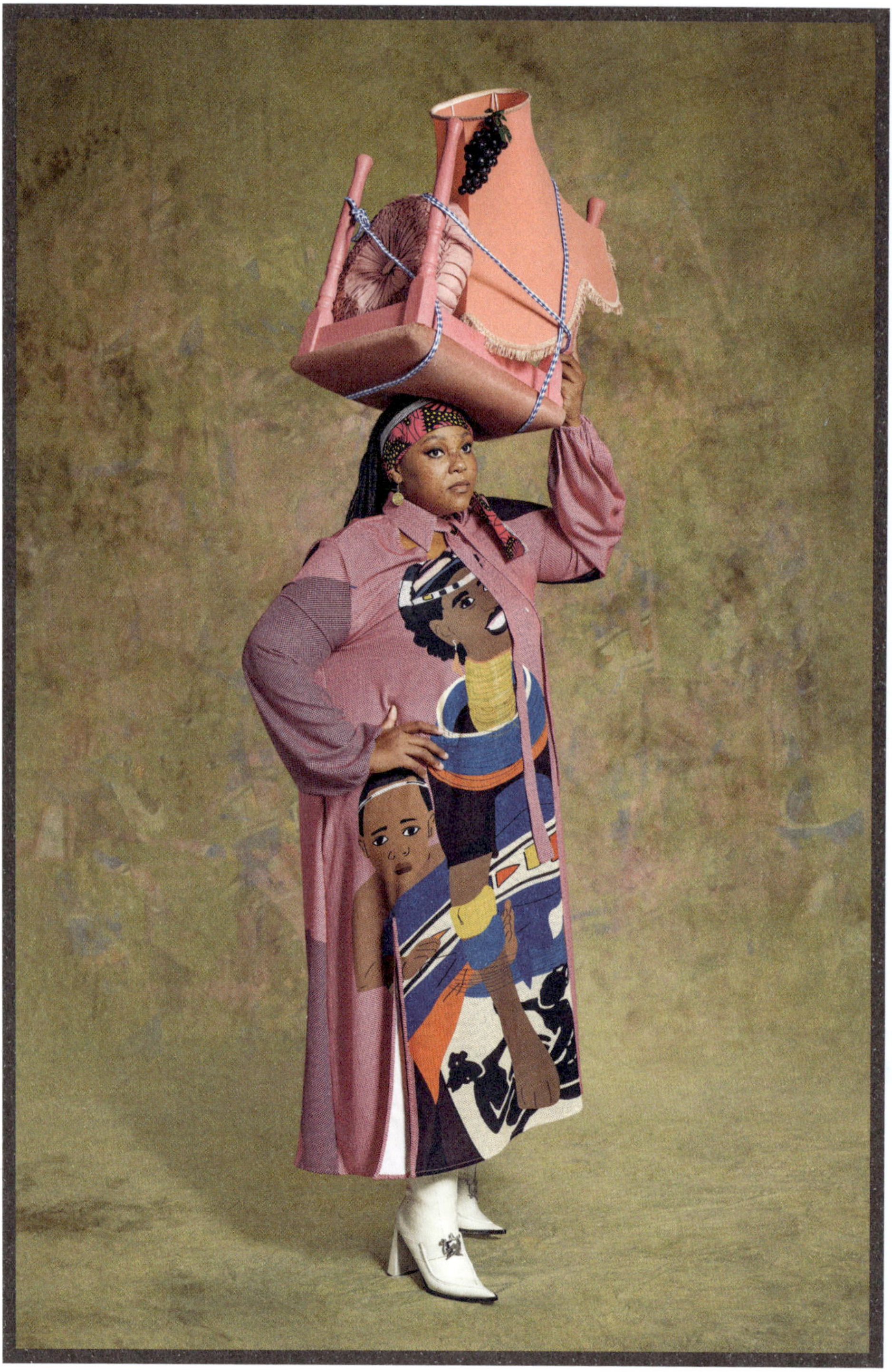

apron, which features a cut along its front hem resembling five scallops aligned next to one another ('itjhorholo'), the attire – one that Esther wears without compromise – presents a powerful totemic look. For me, the silhouette of the Ndebele appears predominantly female-led and female-facing; rather than being conservative, this attire seems to actively rebuff the male gaze, with the body completely enveloped in the 'Nguba' and the limbs inflated by a series of tubular, beaded cuffs. The ornamentation, through beading and accessorization, appears to reflect individual personalities and tastes rather than to be a form of externally motivated peacocking. All this – in whole or in part – has influenced fashion designers both directly and indirectly, including myself.

Early in 2022, I created what is now my annual Heritage Dress Capsule: a series of nine dresses celebrating nine South African cultures. For the Ndebele Dress, I wanted to respectfully reflect the joyful, spirited and complex attire worn by Ndebele women, and my research led to many references both worn by and explored by Dr Esther Mahlangu. In this, she acts as a generous purveyor of her people and their culture, and beautifully funnels this culture into mediums and multi-disciplinary projects that maintain the original reverence of the Ndebele people while still allowing new perspectives about them to take root – especially for an audience far-removed geographically, culturally and socio-economically. Looking at the influence of the Ndebele on a macro scale, we can list a myriad of trends – both past and present – that not only share a commonality with the Ndebele people, but are most likely appropriated from them.

'Luxury' goods have always taken pride in the art of storytelling, craftsmanship, quality and the ability for individual items to be passed down from generation to generation. African craft shares these exact tenets, especially the craft of the Ndebele people, whose full regalia comfortably stands next to the most labour-intensive couture.

Designers who want to lend their collections a sense of 'regality' often use jewelry that takes inspiration from the Ndebele people. For his Dior Spring/Summer 1998 collection, John Galliano presented a rubberized stacked choker that directly references the Ndebele choker ('Idzila'). References to this type of jewelry have featured in countless other designer collections, modelled by figures such as Naomi Campbell in a 2014 shoot for *Interview* magazine by Mert Alas and Marcus Piggott.

Designers and fashion brands have also taken the famed white-paned colour blocks of the Ndebele and reinterpreted them as an AOP (all-over-print) across a variety of styles – from ready-to-wear to footwear. For Spring/Summer 2011, designer Mara Hoffman looked to South Africa and Zimbabwe for inspiration, where the headlining print was a scaled-down iteration of the Ndebele white-framed print across a range of swimwear pieces. Around that time, lauded footwear brand Christian Louboutin was still enjoying the ultra-success of its 'Ulona' 5½-inch heel, which appropriates the Ndebele multi-colour print through a series of dyed suede patches of star white, stage black, dove grey, blood red, cobalt blue, rose pink and a sour green. The shoe is secured to the foot using a series of rubberized gold bands, further referencing the Ndebele 'Idzila'.

The Ndebele have long found themselves on the mood boards of designer studios and luxury Maisons – sadly, without being specifically credited. However, Esther Mahlangu's alliances with the fashion industry serve as a correction to this course: she is from the Ndebele culture, as well as an important guidepost for it, and – unlike those inspired by and at times appropriating the culture of the Ndebele – understands all the nuances and meanings behind every stroke and motif. From her collection with Nike to her limited edition collection of shirts with African Fashion International (AFI), Esther Mahlangu – through her work in fashion – is adding yet another medium via which to share her culture with the world, preserving it through the power of cloth. These items will undoubtedly be passed down from generation to generation, untarnished by the loose approximations of those simply inspired by the Ndebele culture, having been created by a true beacon of that very culture.

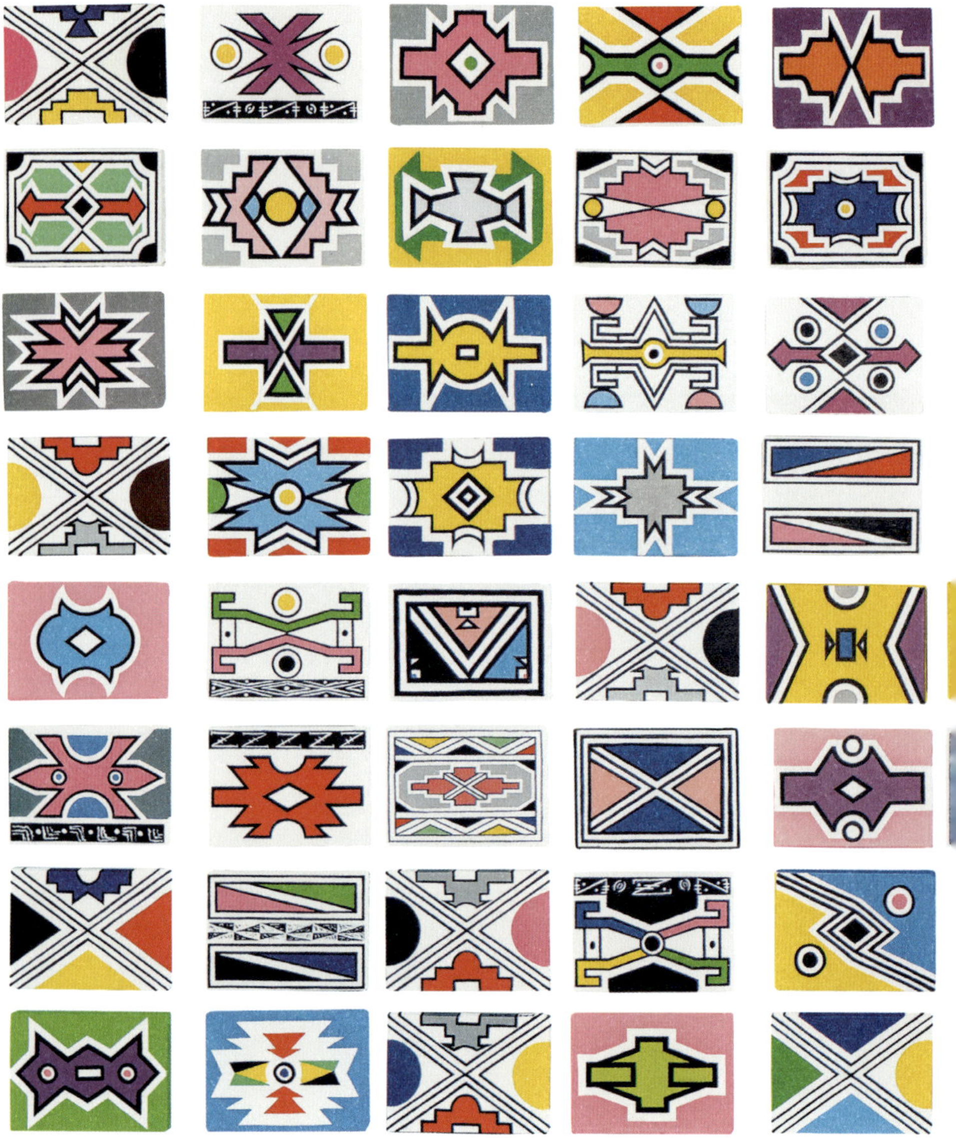

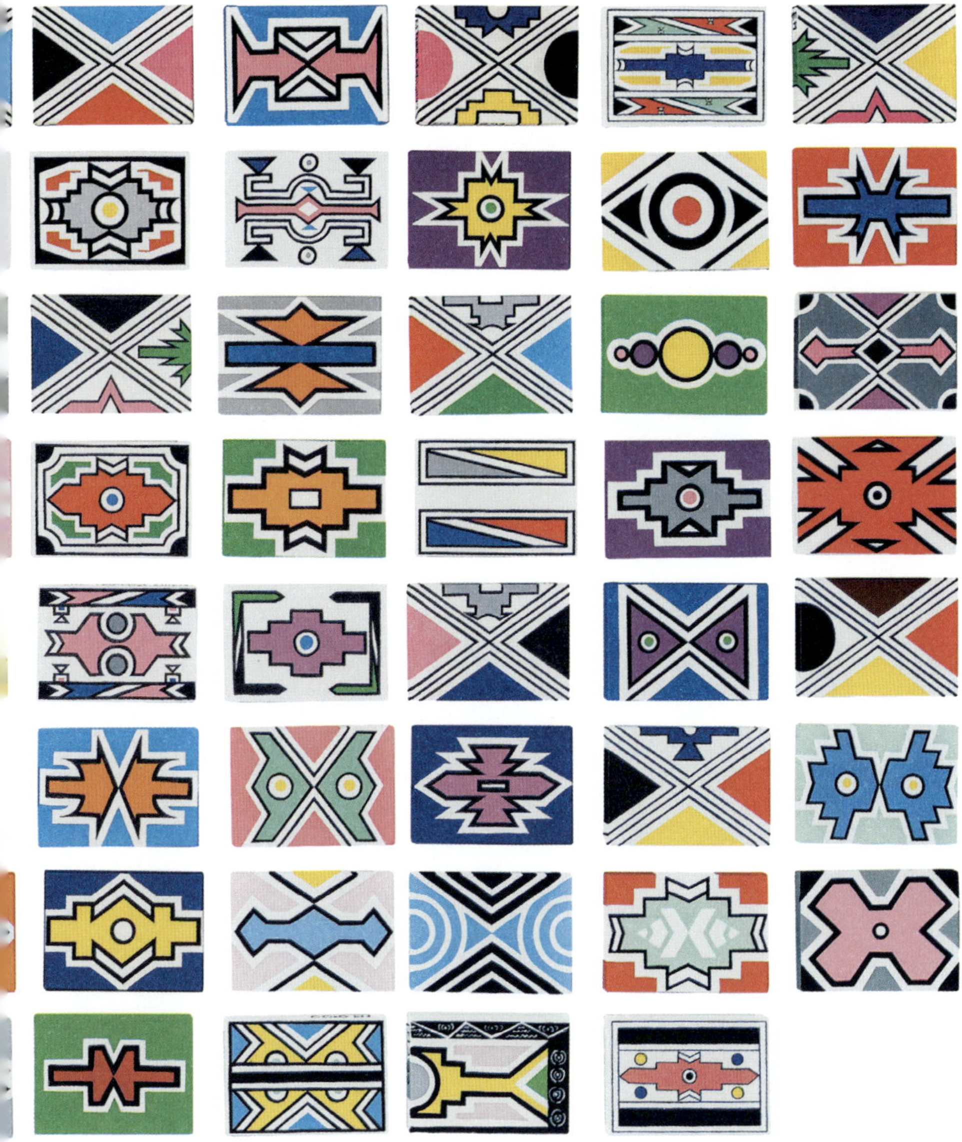

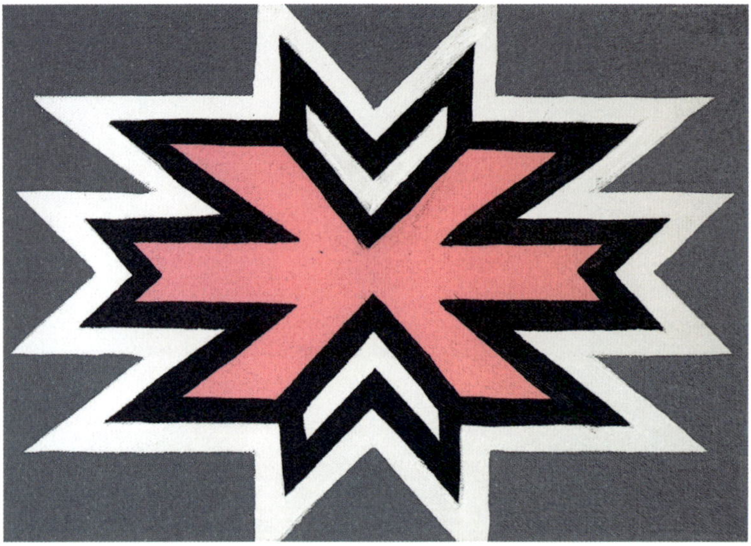

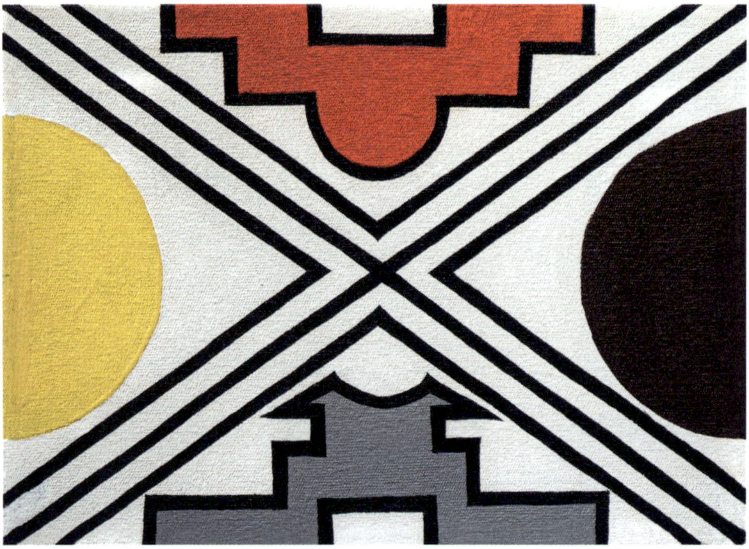

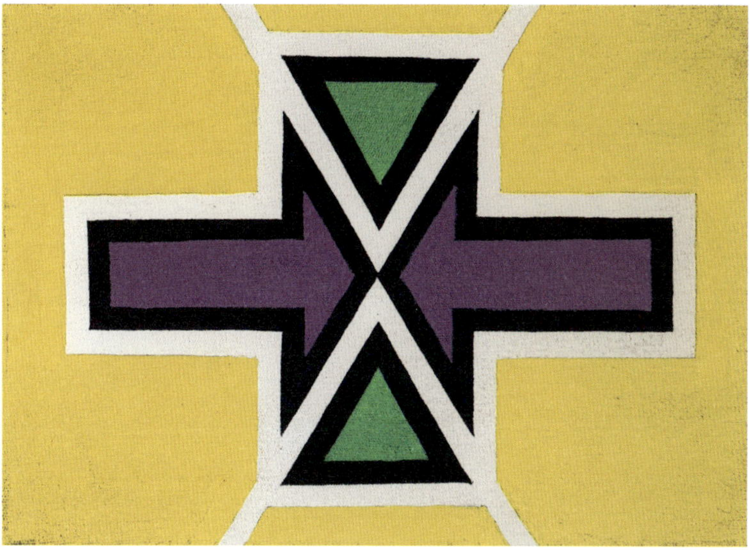

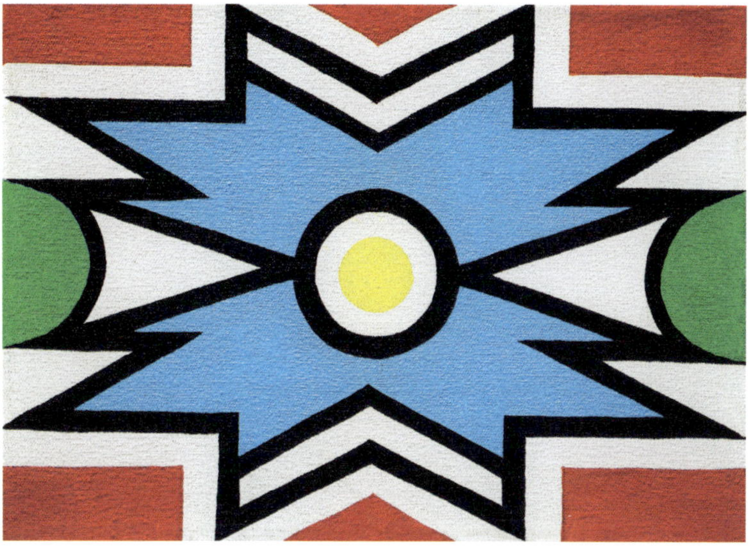

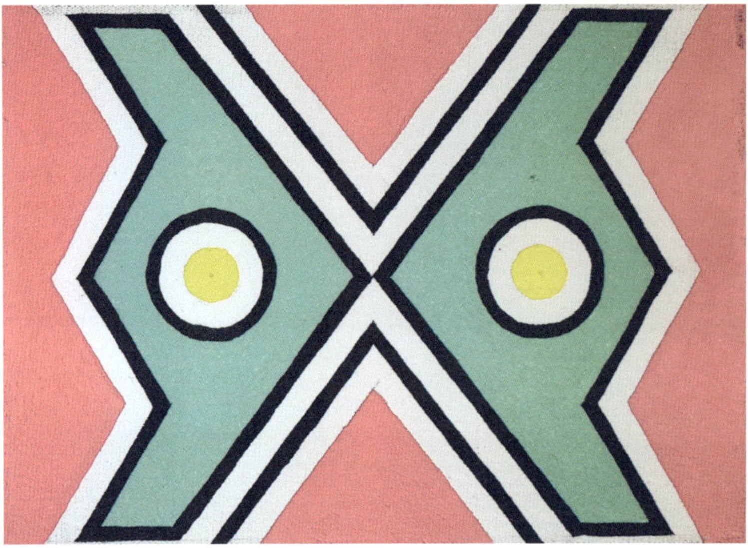

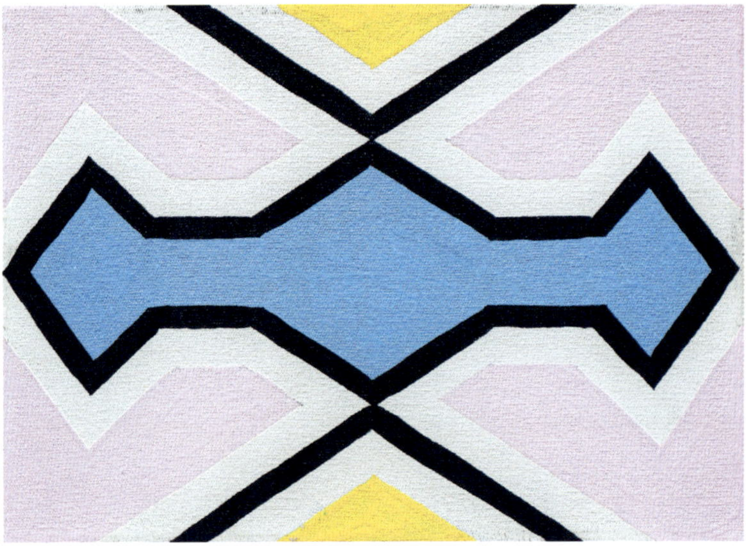

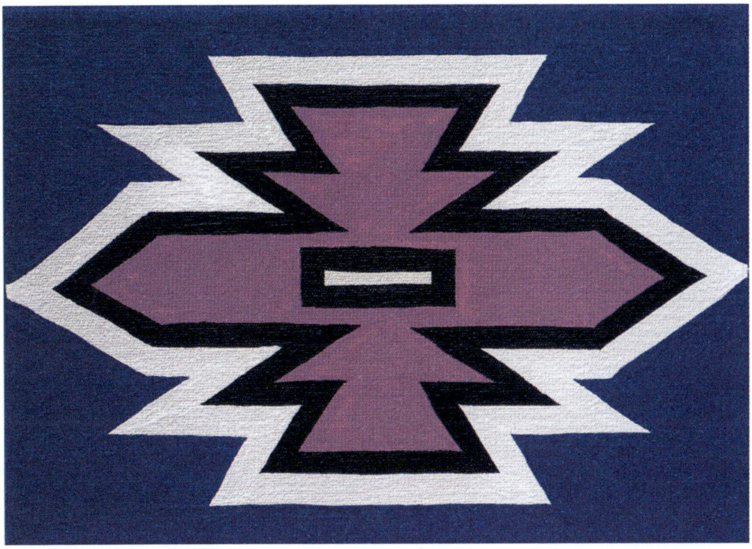

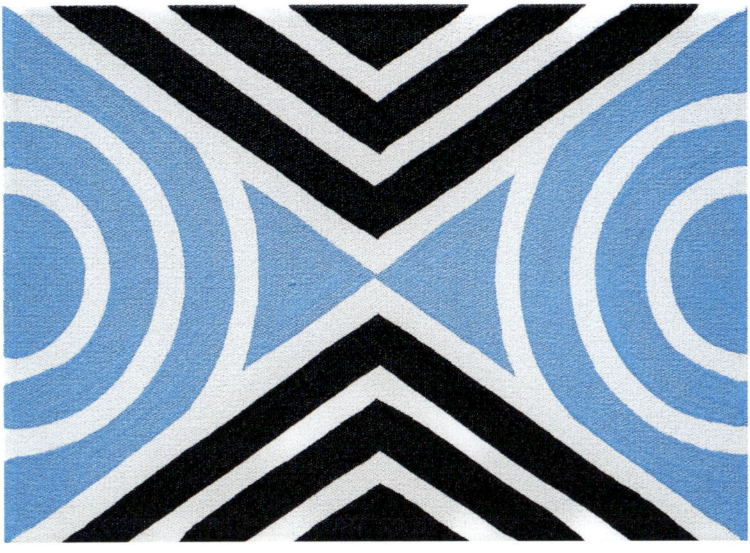

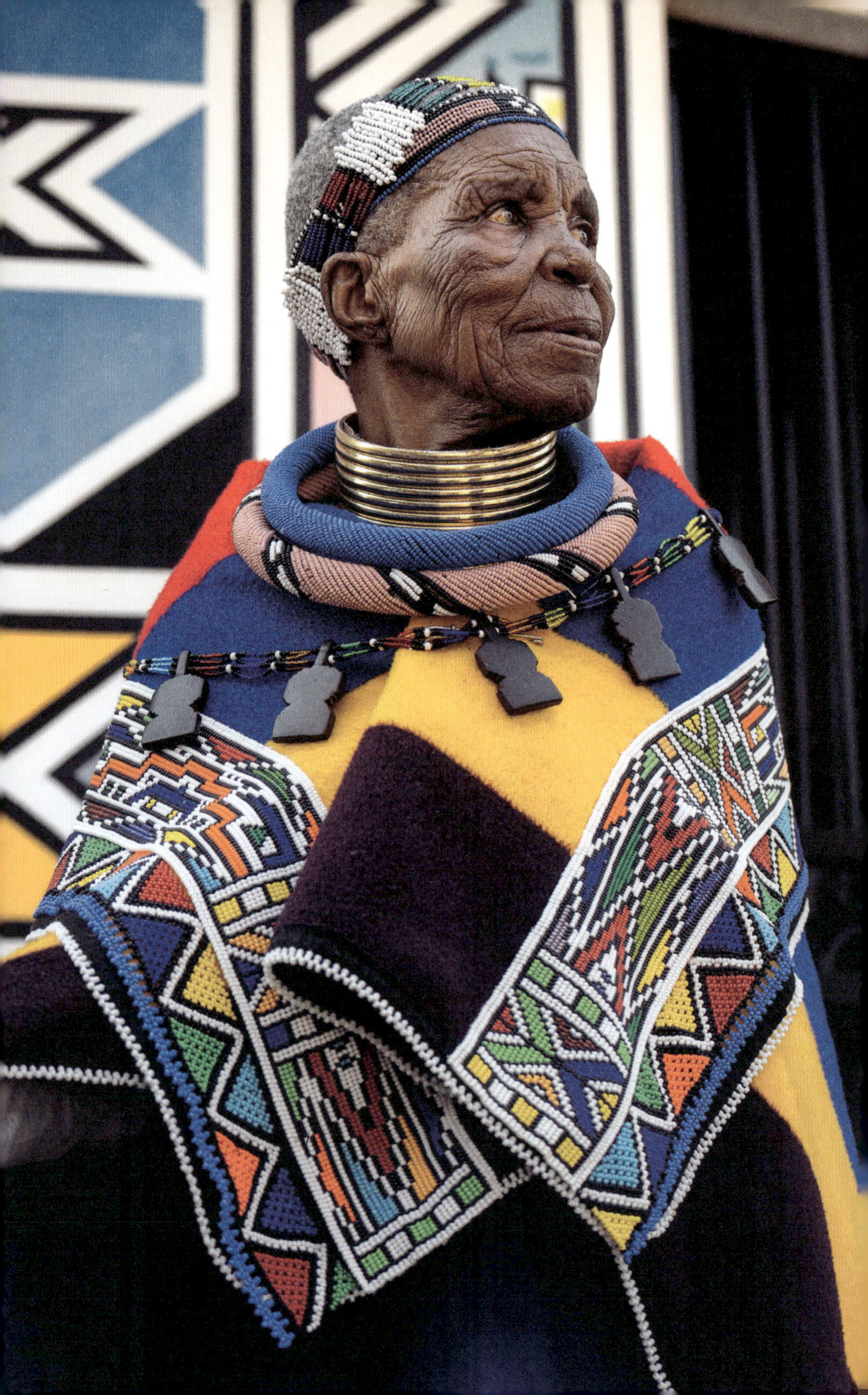

ESTHER MAHLANGU: A BIOGRAPHY

Dr Esther Nostokana Nagiyana Nikwambi Mahlangu (b. 1935, Middelburg, Mpumalanga) is a celebrated South African contemporary artist known for her innovative and boundary-pushing work. Widely recognized as one of the most influential artists and visionaries across generations, Mahlangu began her artistic journey at the age of ten under the guidance of her grandmother and mother, learning the traditional techniques of Ndebele mural painting. Her vibrant geometric artworks build on her cultural heritage, spanning a wide variety of surfaces, found objects and vehicles.

Mahlangu's participation in the group show 'Magiciens de la terre' (Centre Pompidou, Paris, 1989) launched her to international fame. In 1991 she became the first woman artist and African to paint a BMW Art Car, and since then she has collaborated with South African Airways, the Smithsonian Museum, Eytys, Belvedere Vodka, Rolls-Royce and many others.

Mahlangu has exhibited in over twenty countries, sometimes with multiple solo shows. She has created public murals in South Africa, Europe and the United States. Recent solo and group exhibitions include 'Icons of Contemporary Art' at Bellagio Fine Art Gallery (Las Vegas, 2023), 'Art Basel' (with BMW Group, 2023), 'A Force for Change' (Agora Gallery,

New York, 2021), 'Esther Mahlangu 85' (The Melrose Gallery, Johannesburg, 2020) and 'South Africa: The Art of a Nation' (British Museum, London, 2016).

Mahlangu's work is widely sought after by private collectors, and she is represented in over thirty public collections worldwide, including the Centre Pompidou (Paris), Brooklyn Museum (New York), South African National Gallery (Cape Town), Kunstmuseum Bochum (Germany) and the National Museum of Women in the Arts (Washington, DC). Esther Mahlangu is the recipient of numerous honorary doctorates for her contribution to art. In 2019 she was appointed Officer of the French Order of Arts and Letters. She continues her artistic career to this day, and is engaged in teaching traditional Ndebele techniques to younger generations. In 2024 Esther Mahlangu was selected to participate in the 60th International Art Exhibition – 'La Biennale di Venezia', curated by Adriano Pedrosa.

SELECT BIBLIOGRAPHY

100% Africa (Madrid: TF Editores and Guggenheim Museum, Bilbao, 2006)

Bouabré, F.B., 'Sur la Route route d'une mission imprévue', in *Paris la Conscienciеuse: Paris la guideuse du monde* (Paris: Empire & Faro, 2020), pp. 196–204

Courtney-Clarke, M., *Ndebele: The Art of an African Tribe* (London and New York: Thames & Hudson, 1986)

de Jager, F.R. & A.G. Loots, *Esther Mahlangu 2003* (Cape Town: Vgallery, 2003)

de Jager, F.R. & A.G. Loots, *Esther Mahlangu 80* (Cape Town: 34FineArt, 2015)

Duke, L., 'The Living Art of Esther Mahlangu: On a D.C. Street, a South African Master Paints in the Tradition of Her Tribe', *The Washington Post*, 4 September 1994

Elliot, A., *The Ndebele. Art & Culture* (Cape Town: Struik Publishers, 1989)

Esther Mahlangu, Indigenous Lives (Pretoria: Department of Arts and Culture, 2019)

Grenier, C., *Multiple Modernities: 1905–1970* (Paris: Centre Pompidou, 2013)

Lekgoathi, S. & H. Smuts, *Africa meets Africa: Ndebele women designing identity* (Johannesburg: Africa Meets Africa Project, 2008)

Loots, A.G. & F.R. de Jager, *Esther Mahlangu* (Cape Town: UCT Irma Stern Museum, 2003)

Loubser, A., *Recent changes in wall painting amongst the Ndzundza as an indication of social changes amongst AmaNdebele women*, Honours diss. University of the Witwatersrand, Johannesburg, 1994

Magnin, A. & J. Soulillou, *Contemporary Art of Africa* (London: Thames & Hudson, 1996)

Magubane, P. & S. Klopper, *African Heritage, Arts and Crafts* (Cape Town: Struik Publishers, 2001), pp. 44–47

Makhubu, N., 'African Women in Art', in *Oxford Research Encyclopedia of African History* (Oxford: Oxford University Press, 2020)

Marschall, S., 'A Critical Investigation into the Impact of Community Mural Art', *Transformation*, vol. 40, 1999, pp. 55–86

Marschall, S., 'Sites of Identity and Resistance: Urban Community Murals and Rural Wall Decoration in South Africa', *African Arts*, vol. 35, no. 3, 2002, p. 40

New Identities: Zeitgenössische Kunst Aus Südafrika (Ostfildern: Hatje Cantz and Museum Bochum, Germany, 2005)

Van Vuuren, C., 'In memory of the Ndebele homestead: women as earthen builders and mural artists', *South African Journal of Art History*, vol. 30, no. 1, 2015, pp. 141–57

CONTRIBUTOR BIOGRAPHIES

Thomas Girst (b. 1971, Trier, Germany) is a foreign correspondent for *Die Tageszeitung*, and head of the Art Science Research Laboratory under the directorship of Stephen Jay Gould of Harvard University, New York, 1995–2003. Since 2003 he has been the Global Head of Cultural Engagement at the BMW Group and in 2016 he received the 'European Cultural Manager of the Year' award. Girst is honorary professor at the Academy of Fine Arts, Munich. His books have been translated into numerous languages and include: *Art, Literature, and the Japanese American Internment* (2010), *The Duchamp Dictionary* (2014), *BMW Art Cars* (2012), *100 Secrets of the Art World* (2016) and *Alle Zeit der Welt* (2019). In 2027 *Cultural Management: A Global Guide* will be published by Thames & Hudson.

Thebe Magugu (b. 1993, Kimberley, South Africa) is a designer and cultural advocate based in Johannesburg. Magugu studied Fashion Design, Fashion Photography and Fashion Media, all of which play a very important role in his storytelling. His luxury fashion brand, established in 2016, is rooted in the idea of education, acting as an encyclopaedia of stories and craft. In 2019 Magugu won the International Fashion Showcase with the British Fashion Council and the LVMH Prize. He was a finalist for the International Woolmark Prize in 2021. His annual magazine, *Faculty Press*, was named 'the voice of a generation' by *Vogue*. He has collaborated with brands including Dior, Valentino, Spotify and Adidas.

Nontobeko Ntombela (b. 1982, South Africa) works at the Department of Curatorial, Public and Visual Cultures, Wits School of Arts, Johannesburg. Her research focuses on modern and contemporary South African art, with a particular interest in Black women artists. Ntombela previously worked as a curator for organizations including Johannesburg Art Gallery (2010–20) and Durban University of Technology Art Gallery (2005–10). Recent curatorial projects include 'Then I Knew I Was Good at Painting: Esther Mahlangu, A Retrospective' (Iziko South African National Galleries, Cape Town; Wits Art Museum, Johannesburg, 2024–25) and 'When Rain Clouds Gather: South African Black Women Artists 1940–2000' (Norval Foundation, Cape Town, 2022–23). Ntombela has advised organizations including the South African Department of Arts and Culture, Art for Human Rights Trust and the National Arts Council of South Africa.

Pitika Ntuli (b. 1942, Springs, South Africa) is an internationally renowned South African sculptor, poet, cultural activist and academic who spent thirty-two years in exile in Swaziland and the UK. He holds an MFA from the Pratt Institute, New York, and an MA from Brunel University, London. While in exile in the UK he taught Art History and Cultural Studies at four London universities. He has exhibited his sculpture in several individual and group exhibitions and has organized numerous international art and cultural events. Since 2010 Ntuli has created monumental sculptures in Belfast Black granite, recording the culture and historical struggles of South Africa.

Azu Nwagbogu (b. 1975, Lagos, Nigeria) is a curator and writer. He is the founder and Director of the African Artists' Foundation in Lagos, a non-profit organization dedicated to promoting African art and artists. Nwagbogu was Director of the Zeitz Museum of Contemporary Art in South Africa from June 2018 to May 2019. He is also the founder of the LagosPhoto Festival, an annual international photography festival held in Lagos. Nwagbogu is known for his commitment to showcasing the diversity and richness of contemporary African art and culture.

Hans Ulrich Obrist (b. 1968, Zurich, Switzerland) is Artistic Director of Serpentine in London, and Senior Advisor at LUMA Arles. Prior to this, he was the Curator of the Musée d'Art Moderne de la Ville de Paris. Since his first show 'World Soup: Küchenausstellung' (St. Gallen, 1991), he has curated more than 350 shows. Obrist's recent publications include *Ways of Curating* (2015), *The Age of Earthquakes: A Guide to the Extreme Present* (as co-author, 2015), *Lives of the Artists, Lives of Architects* (2015), *140 Ideas for Planet Earth* (as co-author, 2021), *James Lovelock: Ever Gaia* (2023), *Remember to Dream* (2023) and *Une vie in progress* (2023).

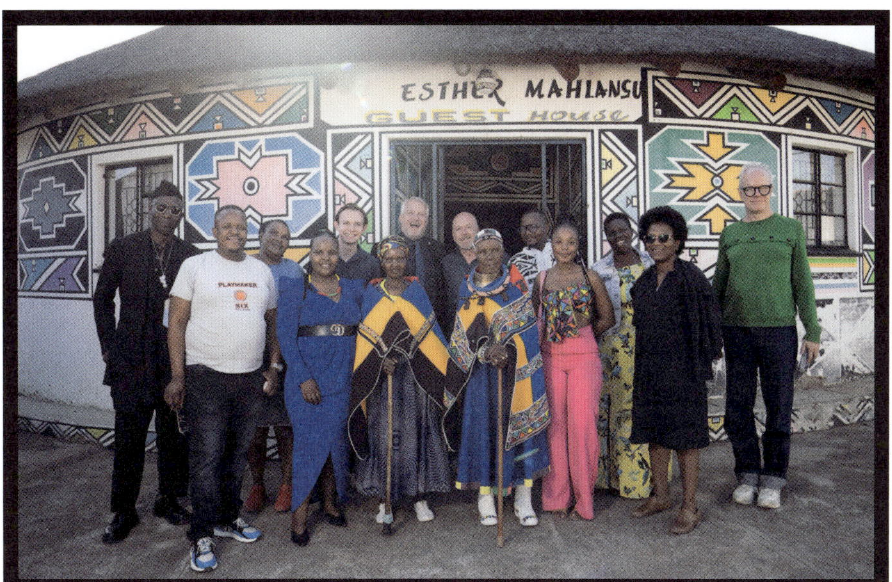

ACKNOWLEDGMENTS

Our heartfelt thanks go to Esther Mahlangu and her family and friends, who have been a cornerstone of support and inspiration. We extend our appreciation to Musa Mahlangu, Betty Mahlangu, Mxolisi Mahlangu, Thabisile Masombuka, Pitika Ntuli, Antoinette Ntuli and Johannah Sindane for their unwavering support and invaluable insights.

We also wish to express our gratitude to several people who have significantly contributed to the project: Princess Ayoola, Adèle Koechlin, Nontobeko Ntombela, Thebe Magugu, Anika Schwartz, Max Shackleton and Lorraine Two. Your dedication has been instrumental in realizing this project.

The Melrose Gallery team has been a pillar of support throughout this journey. We thank Craig Mark, without whom none of this would have ever happened, Donovan Baartman, Mike Boishelo, Shania Mely, Tyron Redman, Ruzy Rusike, Clint Strydom and Liz Willey for their relentless work and vision.

We also wish to convey our appreciation to Larry Warsh and the Mimran Collection.

Special thanks are extended to the Esther Mahlangu Retrospective Exhibition team, whose dedication and expertise have been crucial in showcasing the life and work of Esther Mahlangu. We are grateful to Vidya Chagan, Shruthi Naira and Aarti Shah.

At Thames & Hudson, we extend our gratitude to Mohara Gill, Robert Heath, Michela Parkin, Karolina Prymaka, Roger Thorp, Clare Tillyer and Matthew Watson Young.

On-site efforts were crucial in making the interviews possible. We thank Gavin Benade, Nnana Nkomo, Kevin Sawyer and Rodney Tshidada for their professionalism and dedication. The accuracy and clarity of our content were greatly enhanced by the transcript and translation services of wordinc GmbH and David Vemba.

We acknowledge the contributions of the team at the Looping Group: Lea Burhenne, Dana Ross, Hannah Schell and Anna Schlimok.

The generous support of the BMW Group made this publication possible. We are thankful to Ilka Horstmeier and Maximilian Schöberl, to Peter van Binsbergen, Renier Beneke, Alexander Bilgeri, Stella Clarke, Stefan Clauss, Michelle Dejager, Marcelle Duncan, Bernd Eckstein, Dirk Kaufmann, Angela Konert, Carola Langenhein, Veronika Mance, Thilosh Moodally, Pinky Ndlumbini, Lindsay Pieterse and Eduard Weidenhammer for their enthusiastic participation and patronage.

TEXT CREDITS

p. 6 Hazel Friedman, 'Esther Mahlangu', quoted by Lowery Stokes Sims, 'Esther Mahlangu BMW 525i, 1991', in Thomas Girst (ed.), *BMW Art Cars*, Berlin: Hatje Cantz, 2018, pp. 139–42, p. 142.

p. 16 26 March 2005, transcribed interview responses from BMW.

p. 43 'Esther Mahlangu's BMW Story. A Legacy of Design', 2015,www.youtube.com/watch?v=LX_IyEaaorI (2:58-3:07).

p. 48 Andries Loots and Esther Mahlangu in conversation, 10 May 2003.

p. 55 'In Conversation with Esther Mahlangu', Painting's Not Dead! Issue, *Art Africa*, 9 April 2018, www.artafricamagazine.org/the-painting-s-not-dead-issue-in-conversation-with-esther-mahlangu/

p. 63 'Esther Mahlangu: Ndebele art showed me the world', *NEWS24* interview, 2018, www.youtube.com/watch?v=ozXYBArCfrw (0:22– 0:34).

p. 66 Interview with *Africa Live*, CTGN Africa network, 18 October 2016, www.youtube.com/watch?v=IxD6dvpXig8 (0:44–1:04).

p .71 Andries Loots and Esther Mahlangu in conversation, 10 May 2003.

p. 84 'Titans Documentary: Dr Esther Mahlangu', The Melrose Gallery, Johannesburg, 2020, www.youtube.com/watch?v=bG-SFuRQ8oQ

p. 86 'In Conversation with Esther Mahlangu', Painting's Not Dead! Issue, *Art Africa*, 9 April 2018, www.artafricamagazine.org/the-painting-s-not-dead-issue-in-conversation-with-esther-mahlangu/

p. 94 Valerie Behiery, 'Esther Mahlangu's Gift to the World: The Geometry of Now', *The Art Momentum*, 2020, www.theartmomentum.com/esther-mahlangu/

p. 98 'Esther Mahlangu: Ndebele art showed me the world', *NEWS24* interview, 2018, www.youtube.com/watch?v=ozXYBArCfrw (0:22–0:34).

p. 101 Hannah O'Leary, 'Reinventing Tradition Esther Mahlangu', Sotheby's, 17 February 2017, www.sothebys.com/en/articles/reinventing-tradition-esther-mahlangu

p. 106 'Esther Mahlangu's BMW Story. A Legacy of Design', 2015, www.youtube.com/watch?v=LX_IyEaaorI (2:02–2:22).

p. 123 'Esther Mahlangu, One Of South Africa's Most Famous Artists, Perpetuates Traditional Ndebele Painting', 7 June 2019, www.forbes.com/sites/yjeanmundelsalle/2019/06/07/esther-mahlangu-one-of-south-africas-most-famous-artists-perpetuates-traditional-ndebele-painting/

PICTURE CREDITS

All works in private collections, images courtesy The Melrose Gallery unless otherwise stated. Measurements are given height before width, centimetres followed by inches. All works are untitled and acrylic on canvas unless otherwise stated.

2 (Frontispiece) 2019. 120 × 180 (47¼ × 70⅞)
4 Esther Mahlangu's homestead. Photo: Clint Strydom
7 Esther Mahlangu at work. Photo: Clint Strydom
12 1990. 190 × 124 (74⅞ × 48⅞). Courtesy The Jean Pigozzi African Art Collection
13 1995. 80 × 120 (31½ × 47¼)
14 1991. 190 × 118 (74⅞ × 46½)
15 1990. 190 × 124 (74⅞ × 48⅞). Courtesy The Jean Pigozzi African Art Collection
17 Esther Mahlangu, BMW Art Car, 1991 - BMW 525i, Photo courtesy BMW AG. Photo: Werner Deisenroth
21a (from l to r): Esther Mahlangu, Hans Ulrich Obrist, Azu Nwagbogu and Thomas Girst in conversation. Photo: Clint Strydom
21b Esther Mahlangu. Photo: Clint Strydom
24a Interior view. Photo: Clint Strydom
24b Drawings by Esther Mahlangu on Post-it notes. Courtesy Hans Ulrich Obrist
29 Esther Mahlangu. Photo: Clint Strydom
33 Esther Mahlangu. Photo: Clint Strydom
34–35 2001. 200 × 480 (78¾ × 189)
36, 37 2009. 102.5 × 134 (40⅜ × 52⅞)
38 2010.177 90 × 120 (35½ × 47¼)
39 2010. 90 × 120 (35½ × 47¼)
40–41 2010. 90 × 120 (35½ × 47¼)
42, 43 2010. 87.5 × 120.5 (34½ × 47½)
44 2010. 75 × 89.5 (29⅝ × 35¼)
45 2010. 64.5 × 97.5 (25½ × 38½)
46–47 2010. 192.90 × 120.5 (35½ × 47½)
48 2010. 55.5 × 95 (21⅞ × 37½)
49 2010. 63.5 × 93 (25 × 36⅞)
50–51a 2010. 200 × 720 (78¾ × 283½)
50–51b 2010. 180 × 600 (70⅞ × 236¼)
52 2010. 106 × 156 (41¾ × 61½)
53 2011. 70.5 × 87.5 (3 × 34½)
54, 55 2011. 49.5 × 70 (19½ × 27⅝)
56–57 2011. 89 × 110 (35⅛ × 43⅜)
58a, 59 2011. 90.5 × 120.5 (35¾ × 47½)
58b 2011. 89.5 × 120 (35¼ × 47¼)
60–61 2011. 50 × 70 (19¾ × 27⅝)
62, 63 2011. 50 × 70 (19¾ × 27⅝)
64–65 2011. 50.5 × 70.5 (20 × 27⅞)
67a 2011. 90 × 110 (35½ × 43⅜)
67b 2012. 69.5 × 89.5 (27⅜ × 35¼)
68–69 2012. 50 × 70 (19¾ × 27⅝)
70, 71 2012. 50 × 70 (19¾ × 27⅝)
72–73 2012. 50 × 70 (19¾ × 27⅝)
74–75 2016. 106 × 154 (41¾ × 60¾). Courtesy Esther Mahlangu/The Melrose Gallery
76 2018. 120 × 180 (47¼ × 70⅞). Courtesy Esther Mahlangu/The Melrose Gallery
77 2018. 100 × 150 (39⅜ × 59⅛)
78–79 2018, 126 × 186 (49⅝ × 73¼). Courtesy Esther Mahlangu/The Melrose Gallery
80 2018. 120 × 120 (47¼ × 47¼). Courtesy Esther Mahlangu/The Melrose Gallery
81 2018. 120 × 120 (47¼ × 47¼). Courtesy Esther Mahlangu/The Melrose Gallery
82, 83 2019. 100 × 150 (39⅜ × 59⅛)
85a 2019. 100 × 150 (39⅜ × 59⅛)
85b 2019. 70 × 100 (27⅝ × 39⅜). Courtesy Esther Mahlangu/ The Melrose Gallery
87 2019. 120 × 120 (47¼ × 47¼). Collection Paul Berman, Paul Berman Brothers

88–89 2019. 120×180 (47¼×70⅞). Justin Divaris Collection
90, 91 2019. 120×180 (47¼×70⅞).
92–93 2020. 70×100 (27⅝×39⅜). Courtesy Esther Mahlangu/The Melrose Gallery
95 2020. 100×100 (39⅜×39⅜). Courtesy Esther Mahlangu/The Melrose Gallery
96–97 2020. 240×360 (94½×141¾), panel piece. Courtesy Esther Mahlangu/The Melrose Gallery
99 2020. 120×120 (47¼×47¼). Courtesy Esther Mahlangu/The Melrose Gallery
100 2020. 180 (70⅞) in diameter
102–103 2020. 92×122 (36¼×48⅛). Courtesy Esther Mahlangu/The Melrose Gallery
104, 105 2021. 120×180 (47¼×70⅞). Courtesy Esther Mahlangu/The Melrose Gallery
107 2021. 120×120 (47¼×47¼). Courtesy Esther Mahlangu/The Melrose Gallery
108 2021. 70×100 (27⅝×39⅜). Corporate Collection
109 2021. 100×150 (39⅜×59⅛) Courtesy Esther Mahlangu/The Melrose Gallery
110, 111 2022. 180 (70⅞) in diameter. Courtesy Esther Mahlangu/The Melrose Gallery
112–113 2022. 120 × 180 (47¼×70⅞). Collection Alma Trades FZ LLC
114 2023. 70×100 (27⅝×39⅜). Courtesy Esther Mahlangu/The Melrose Gallery
115 2023. 120×120 (47¼×47¼). Courtesy Esther Mahlangu/The Melrose Gallery
116–117 2023. 120×180 (47¼×70⅞). Courtesy Esther Mahlangu/The Melrose Gallery
120a 2021. Acrylic on GRP, 20×40 (7⅞×15¾)
120b 2021. Acrylic on GRP, 30×40 (11⅞×15¾). Courtesy Esther Mahlangu/The Melrose Gallery
121a 2021. Acrylic on GRP, 20×40 (7⅞×15¾). Courtesy Esther Mahlangu/The Melrose Gallery
121b 2021. Acrylic on GRP, 30×40 (11⅞×15¾)
124 Ndebele Heritage Dress Photo: Aart Verrips, Styling: Chloe Andrea Welgemoed
128–129 *87 Gestures*, 2022. Installation, acrylic on canvas. 87 pieces, each 20×30 (7⅞×11⅞). Collection Ben Milstein
130a 2019 (*87 Gestures*, detail)
130b 2019 (*87 Gestures*, detail)
131a 2019 (*87 Gestures*, detail)
131b *Ndebele Abstract*, 2022 (*87 Gestures*, detail)
132a *Ndebele Abstract*, 2022 (*87 Gestures*, detail)
132b 2022 (*87 Gestures*, detail)
133a 2019 (*87 Gestures*, detail)
133b 2022 (*87 Gestures*, detail)
134 Esther Mahlangu. Photo: Clint Strydom
139 Esther Mahlangu (centre) with (from l to r): Azu Nwagbogu, Musa Mahlangu, Zodwa Masango, Betty Mahlangu, Eduard Weidenhammer, Johana Sidane, Thomas Girst, Craig Mark, Xoli Mahlangu, Thabisile Masombuka, Thembi Sindane, Nontobeko Ntombela and Hans Ulrich Obrist. Photo courtesy BMW AG.

Case: *Untitled*, 2019. Acrylic on canvas, 120 × 180 (47¼ × 70⅞). Justin Divaris Collection.

Endpapers: *Untitled*, 2020. Acrylic on canvas, 70 × 100 (27⅝ × 39⅜). Courtesy Esther Mahlangu/The Melrose Gallery; *Untitled*, 2019. Acrylic on canvas, 70 × 100 (27⅝ × 39⅜). Courtesy Private Collection.

First published in the United Kingdom in 2024 by Thames & Hudson Ltd, 181A High Holborn, London WC1V 7QX

First published in the United States of America in 2024 by Thames & Hudson Inc., 500 Fifth Avenue, New York, New York 10110

Reprinted 2024

Designed by Karolina Prymaka
Coordinating Editor: Eduard Weidenhammer

British Library Cataloguing-in-Publication Data
A catalogue record for this book is available from the British Library

Library of Congress Control Number 2024932537

ISBN 978-0-500-02812-4

Printed in China by RR Donnelley

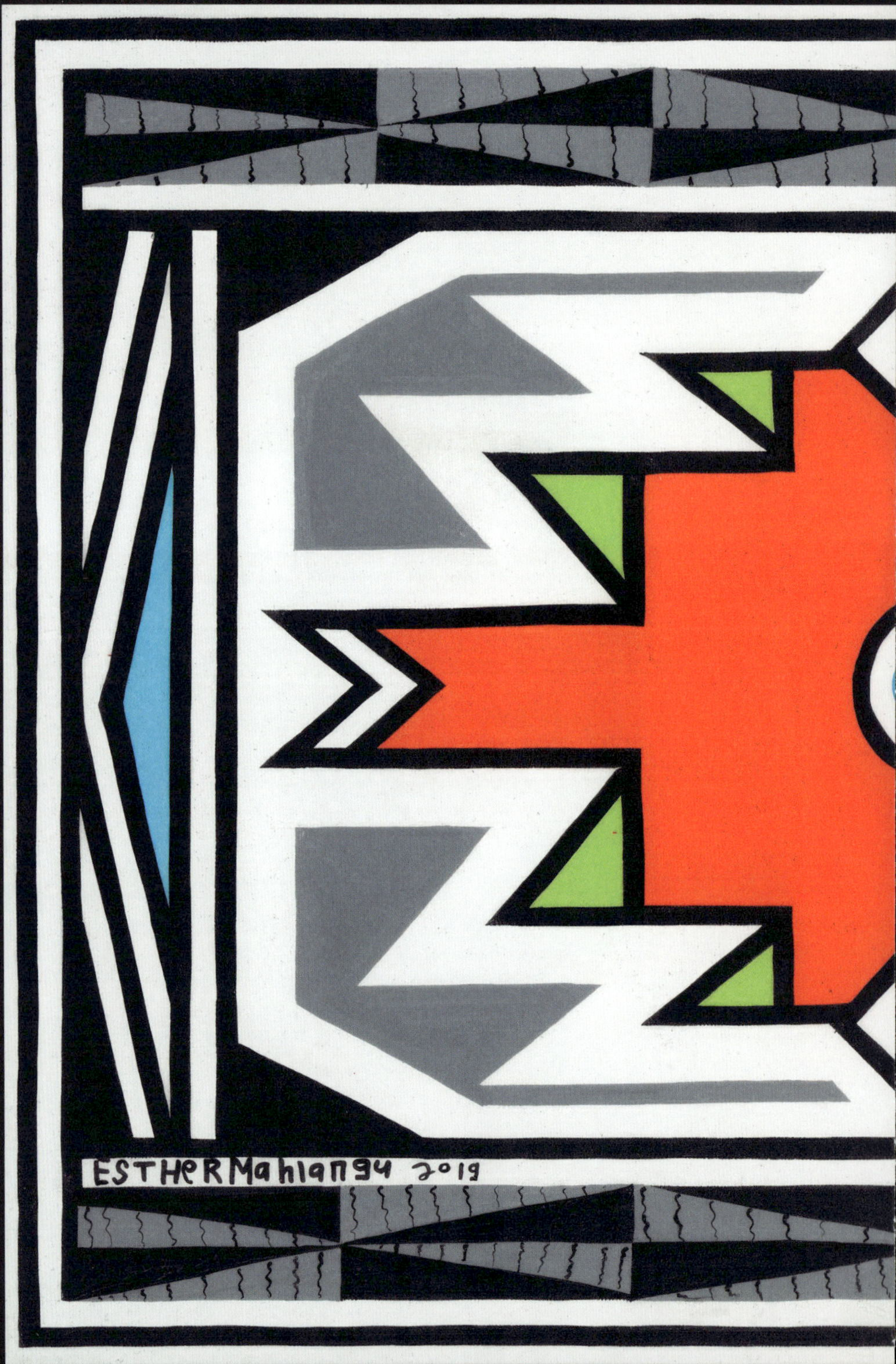
ESTHeR Mahlangu 2019